OPTICAL
PATTERN RECOGNITION
USING HOLOGRAPHIC TECHNIQUES

ELECTRONIC SYSTEMS ENGINEERING SERIES

Consulting Editor   **E L Dagless**
University of Bristol

OTHER TITLES IN THE SERIES

Advanced Microprocessor Architectures   *L Ciminiera and A Valenzano*

Modern Logic Design   *D Green*

Data Communications, Computer Networks and OSI (2nd Edn.)   *F Halsall*

Microwave Components and Systems   *K F Sander*

OPTICAL
PATTERN RECOGNITION
USING HOLOGRAPHIC TECHNIQUES

Neil Collings
STC Technology Ltd

Addison-Wesley Publishing Company

Wokingham, England • Reading, Massachusetts • Menlo Park, California
New York • Don Mills, Ontario • Amsterdam • Bonn
Sydney • Singapore • Tokyo • Madrid • San Juan

Cover design by Crayon Design, Henley-on-Thames.
Typeset by Colset Private Limited, Singapore.
Printed in Great Britain by The Bath Press, Avon.

First printed 1988.

British Library Cataloguing in Publication Data
Collings, Neil
    Optical pattern recognition using holographic techniques.
    1. Pattern perception
    I. Title
    621.39′9   Q327

    ISBN 0–201–14549–9

Library of Congress Cataloguing in Publication Data
Collings, Neil.
    Optical pattern recognition using holographic techniques.

    Bibliography: p.
    Includes index.
    1. Optical pattern recognition.   2. Holography.
I. Title.
TA1650.C64   1988   621.39′9   87–27062
ISBN 0–201–14549–9

This book is dedicated to my wife, Lydia, who has encouraged me from its initiation through to its completion.

PREFACE

I arrived in the field of holographic pattern recognition three years ago. Although I had a solid basis in optics, the field itself was new to me. However, it was sufficiently well circumscribed for me to understand it quickly, and this enabled me to act as tutor to my colleagues. They had a multiplicity of backgrounds, coming from such diverse areas as displays technology, machine vision, instrumentation and technical management. In addition, I had the benefit of a research student who was a computer scientist, and who asked me to detail my arguments at every instance. This book, which is the result of my experience, is intended to provide a systematic account of optical design.

Historically, the story of Fourier optics began in the 1940s when, as a result of using mathematics to describe the behaviour of light, it was appreciated that light could be used to perform mathematical transformations. In particular, the facility with which a Fourier transformation could be performed by a lens was underlined. The leader in this field was Duffieux whose ideas have been translated into English in [1]. Surprisingly, it was not until the advent of the laser that the technological import of this began to be exploited, and its continued development depends, to a certain extent, on the production of more compact laser systems. However, the cohesion and success of this exploitation have depended on the use of the Fourier transform property of lenses.

Overview

The book assumes no prior knowledge of optics on the part of the reader, and therefore the essentials are outlined in Chapter 2. Most graduates in numerate disciplines should be comfortable here, although those sections explaining the Fourier transform properties of a lens, Sections 2.3 to 2.5, can be omitted. Chapter 3 details the optical engineering calculations that must be performed by anyone wishing to build a correlator. These will allow the reader to become skilled at 'scratch-pad' calculations. Further system elaborations have been deferred to Chapter 6. A Glossary has been included as a reference for commonly used terms.

To evaluate the scope of pattern recognition using holography, it is important to have an idea of what is practicable in the way of devices for optical systems. Two chapters are devoted to a description of current devices (and device concepts): Chapter 4 treats the devices used to input the pattern into the optical system, and Chapter 5 treats those that are used to record the hologram of the pattern. The shortage of good devices is the greatest impediment to the accelerated use of optical systems in simple pattern recognition problems, although the systems do seem to be remarkably tolerant of device imperfections. However, device development is expensive and not always successful. Perhaps those involved in device physics will read this book and gain a better understanding of the requirements of such optical systems.

This book has been written in the belief that parallel optical processing – that is, the processing of information written across an optical wavefront – will play a future role in information processing, especially when the information is in the form of images. Although this study is focussed on one particular form of processing – namely, the analogue Fourier transform – the principles and devices can be carried over into more general optical computing systems, such as the development of neural net processors based on holography [2]. Unfortunately, optical computing must develop in the shadow of powerful electronic computing systems, which reduces resources and, more importantly, colours the thinking of the system architects. More fertile imagination is required to harness the power of optics, and it is hoped that this book may give to the people with a lay interest in optical computing a feel for the practicalities of optical devices and systems.

The fundamental principles of optical processing have been described in books by Casasent [3], Goodman [4] and Lee [5]. Here, however, the subject matter is treated on a more practical level, in part to convey the message to the reader that these systems can and are being built. A major part of the activity in this field is carried out by the American Department of Defense, and much of the published work is also American. However, there has been a major UK initiative during the past three years to develop the kind of devices required for these systems. This has been funded by the Department of Trade and Industry, of which the author has been a beneficiary, and some of the work carried out under this scheme is described in the appendix.

Using the book

Some universities have recognized that there is an insufficient supply of graduates with training in optics and are providing appropriate postgraduate courses. The subject matter of this book could provide some material for such courses. Alternatively, it might be introduced into a degree course as an applications study for Fourier optics. The technical aspects of optical system design stand in relation to the mathematics of physical optics rather like electronics stands in relation to the theory of semiconductor junctions. There are a number of optical component manufacturers who furnish equipment for undergraduate experiments in holography and it is possible to press modern liquid crystal displays into service as input devices [6]. Hence, it should be possible, with some ingenuity, to produce interesting undergraduate experiments.

On the industrial front, there are a range of opinions expressed about optical processing. A number of people are aware of its long gestation period and that the renewed interest of 25 years ago was contingent on the development of the laser. However, the lack of devices has hampered its continued evolution. Others have more basic arguments about the inflexibility of the pattern match. Their attention is drawn to Chapter 6 where this problem is addressed. The most percipient recognize that this whole technology will be very expensive to develop. Although the aim is to produce systems that are more compact, cheaper and consume less power than their electronic counterparts, and although there are currently cheap devices to do the job, a full scale initiative in this area must involve large sums of money. An attempt has been made to lay out the case fairly in this book, and not overstate the case for the optical alternative.

Acknowledgements

I would like to thank STC for allowing me the time to write this book, and the secretarial and drawing office support to produce it. Furthermore, I express my appreciation to the reviewers, in particular Professor Maurice Beck, and to Dave Armitage and Robin Scarr for suggesting corrections.

Neil Collings
November 1987

CONTENTS

CHAPTER 1
INTRODUCTION

1.1 General introduction

This chapter aims to introduce the reader to the field of pattern recognition. Its primary concern is to present the nature of the thinking involved, as optics will play an increasingly important role in parallel processing systems. The reason for this is that parallel data flow and synchronicity are natural properties of an expanded light beam: the elements of a pattern encoded on a beam by, for example, a mask, all arrive at the same time at the several planes of the optical system through which the beam passes. Such behaviour is in marked contrast to an electronic processing system where the natural data flow is one dimensional. Furthermore, such parallel architectures have major synchronization problems. Although the application of optics has been impeded by the lack of suitable hardware, a number of laboratories are now working on spatial light modulators with the aim of developing:

- devices for inputting the data in parallel format,
- holographic recording materials, which record and erase at speeds commensurate with fast processing, and
- arrays of bistable devices, which process the elements of the data array in parallel.

1

The first two types of device are of direct relevance to analogue pattern recognition and are the subject of Chapters 4 and 5, respectively.

1.2   Overview of pattern recognition techniques

Although a number of pattern recognition strategies are available, we will only consider the two major techniques here; namely, **template matching** and **feature extraction** (Figure 1.1). In the simplest sense, template matching refers to the comparison of the test pattern with a number of stored patterns until an exact match is found. It is a top-down process in the sense that the trial procedure does not depend on the test pattern in any way. On the other hand, feature extraction starts from the test pattern and measures a limited number of features that are known, in advance, to be good descriptors for the pattern. This is a data-driven bottom-up process. As we shall see, the sharp distinction between these two approaches is lost in more complex cases.

Template matching is both computationally and memory intensive when all but the simplest patterns are considered. In addition, it is sensitive to the exact location of the object, unless autocorrelation techniques are used. However, this kind of computation can be performed quickly using optical techniques, as the rest of the book will show. In the case of more complex patterns – for example, where the orientation of a three-dimensional object is uncertain and a number of two-dimensional perspectives must be combined – some form of generalized template matching is required, so that the stored images are an averaged version of a number of templates. Statistical decision theory helps in the mathematical construction of the generalized template and the recognition analysis.

The computational and memory requirements of feature extraction are less severe than template matching, and a number of systems based on microcomputers and frame stores have been developed for low-level vision tasks. At an intermediate level, minicomputers are employed; for example, to generate the Fourier descriptors of the perimeter lines in a silhouette of the pattern. For higher level tasks, artificial intelligence techniques would be used, for example, in analyzing the syntax (or elucidating the manner in which the features connect together) of skeleton images. The fundamental problem with feature extraction is that important information may be lost in the extensive data reduction at the pre-processing stage. In computational tasks where the data rate is high, this stage has been identified as the one requiring the greatest computing power. However, specialized computer architectures have been developed for high throughput. Two that have been widely used in this particular field are the **systolic array processor** and the **SIMD processor.** In the systolic processor, the data flow is arranged so that each item (for example, a pixel) passes through a sequence of **processing elements (PEs),** each of which perform a given step of the calculation. The speed advantage of this type of processor derives from the property that while

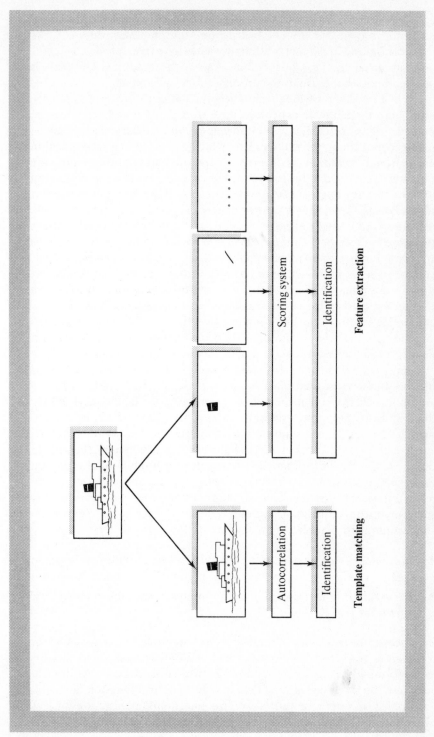

Figure 1.1   Alternative approaches to pattern recognition.

one PE is processing one pixel, other PEs are busy with other pixels. On the other hand, in the SIMD (Single Instruction Multiple Data) processor, the PEs are configured in parallel, so that the same step of the calculation is performed on each pixel of a segment of the image at the same time. The image is segmented because the size of the processor array is limited.

When machine-learning techniques for pattern recognition are considered, both the template matching and feature extraction schemes can be improved. In the first case, *a priori* information about the test pattern can be used to generate an optimized template, which will result in a generalization of the pattern recognition process (see Chapter 6) and may even reduce the burden on memory storage. In the second case, the machine may develop feature vectors for optimized discrimination based on the unprocessed test pattern. For example, the WISARD system [7] employs feature detectors (small groups of pixels) for the interrogation of a replica of the test pattern that is stored in memory. By the parallel interrogation of a number of stores of the test pattern with different feature vectors, and using a voting system, the performance is improved. It may be argued that the conversion of the test pattern into a binary replica is a form of pre-processing, but this is just a limitation imposed by the hardware that is available (silicon RAMs).

Optical technology has found application in the field of pattern recognition, initially, with the optical correlator systems, which perform template matching. Both coherent and incoherent techniques have been developed. The coherent systems are more exacting, in that the optical quality of the devices used must be high. However, these systems have a greater potential than the incoherent ones, where lower quality devices may be used and very low cost systems have been developed. It will be demonstrated in Chapter 2 that a simple lens system generates the two-dimensional Fourier transform of a pattern on the light beam transmitted by the lens. In addition, it will be shown that the transform of a product of two pattern transforms is equivalent to the cross-correlation of the two patterns. Therefore, an optical cross-correlator has a simple architecture and can be readily implemented with static input patterns. The advantages of the cross-correlation technique for template matching are that:

- the match is independent of the test pattern location (shift invariance), and
- the signal-to-noise ratio (SNR) is optimum for detection in white noise situations [8].

Its handicap is the lack of real-time devices for inputting the patterns, and for recording the product of the Fourier transforms of test and stored patterns prior to forming the cross-correlation. The further penetration of this technology into the machine-learning field may be in optical threshold units [9], holographic associative memory [10] or in connectionist architectures such as the Boltzmann machine, which is described in Case Study 1 (Section 1.3). The

Table 1.1 Pattern recognition techniques and selected applications.

Technique	Application
Digital image processing	Visual inspection; character recognition; fingerprint identification
Learning machine	Car number plate identification
Coherent optical processor	Satellite imagery; missile guidance
Incoherent optical processor	Printed circuit board inspection

future contribution to feature extraction techniques could be in the development of optical cellular logic arrays with greater connectivity than present day arrays [11].

1.3 Applications survey

To place the optical correlator technology in perspective, with regard to the other techniques that have been mentioned, examples of the application areas of each are listed in Table 1.1. Although this classification is somewhat arbitrary, it is intended to illustrate that correlators perform well in natural scene environments, and that optical correlators are particularly useful in situations where there is a high information content in the pattern, or where low weight and power consumption are required. Feature extraction techniques are appropriate in those cases where the environment can be tailored (for example, lighting conditions, typewriter letter font, etc.). The following two case studies, in areas of high technological importance, contrast somewhat with this argument, but provide a more detailed comparison of template matching and feature extraction.

CASE STUDY 1: SPEECH ANALYSIS

This application (see Figure 1.2) differs from image recognition tasks with respect to the comparatively low data rate (64 kbit/s compared with 100 Mbit/s for video images). Therefore, the pre-processing stage can be performed with relatively modest computing power. In a current program [12], a feature vector of 18 components is produced at 10 ms intervals. This feature vector then forms the basis for a number of intelligent classification algorithms, which is where the bulk of computing power is deployed. The scores that result from the classification stage are then available for higher levels of understanding, if these are required. It is envisaged that a digital signal processor chip would perform the initial fast Fourier analysis and feed into a microprocessor array for the classification stage.

For the application of optical processing techniques, the speech data is converted to two-dimensional format, and a number of techniques have been described for generating spectrograms (or frequency/time spectra) [13–15]. This is a symbolic representation of the data and it might be regarded as a form of pre-processing. However, it is better viewed as a transformation of the data to a more compact form (because it is a one-dimensional Fourier transformation), which improves the efficiency of the optical processor. The spectrograms are forwarded to an optical system that performs cross-correlations, and the similarity of test and stored patterns can be measured quantitatively in the correlation plane [15].

In both of the preceding techniques, there is no referral between data processed at one time and that processed at another time. In the Boltzmann machine approach [16], there is a mechanism by which past associations can influence present ones, and therefore the context can be used to assist recognition. The Boltzmann machine is an example of a connectionist architecture, where the processing power resides in the multiplicity and strength of interconnections between simple threshold logic units. The strengths of the interconnections are determined by a relaxation method on test data. Of the tasks possible with this approach, one is the detection of the formant frequencies; that is, those frequencies at which the acoustic energy peaks. The sound can then be characterized unambiguously from the first two or three formant frequencies.

This application area is dominated by the feature extraction approach because template matching techniques are inappropriate due to the variability of the data.

CASE STUDY 2: DOCUMENT READER

The complexity of character recognition increases markedly as we move from well-printed, fixed font to poorly printed, variable font typescript. The template matching approach is applicable at the former extreme, of which direct image subtraction methods are particularly appropriate. As the condition of the print deteriorates, it is more advantageous to use a cross-correlation approach, provided that the noise is random. However,

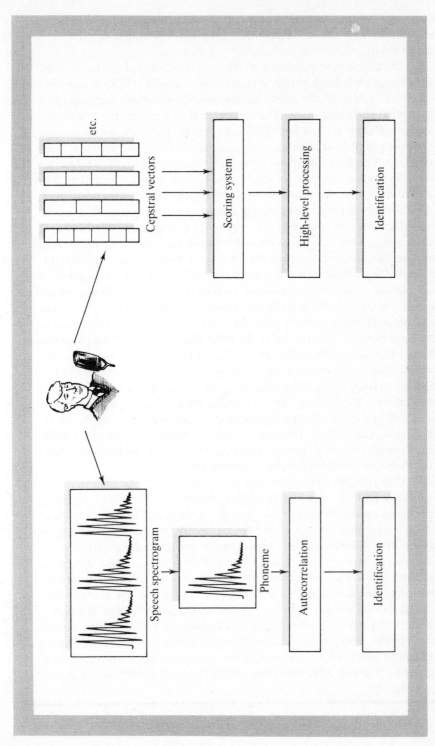

Figure 1.2 Speech analysis.

when there is some systematic break-up of the printed character or when variable font is used, then the template matching approach is inappropriate.

The alternative technique of feature extraction is used in commercial systems. A typical optical character recognition (OCR) system (see Figure 1.3) performs the following operations: scanning, segmentation, registration and recognition. The scanner in such systems may be a photodiode or CCD array, or a line of 20 solar cells [17]. A dedicated processor of limited parallelism is linked to the scanner in expensive systems; alternatively, a standard mainframe computer can be used [18]. Techniques have also been developed for dealing with poor quality print [19]. The speed of these machines can reach several hundred characters per second.

To improve the speed of OCR machines, the parallelism of the input stage must be increased. By way of illustration, consider a system that is simple, but has never been developed due to device limitations. Suppose that a transparency of an A4 page is illuminated by a coherent, collimated light beam and the transmitted light focussed. A property of the focussing, which will be demonstrated later, is that the spatial position of the characters on the page is transformed to phase information at the focal plane (Fourier transformation). Therefore, all the characters of a particular type are superposed at the focal plane. Suppose that there is a pixellated shutter with sufficient resolution that, for any given shutter pattern, only one character type is transmitted. If this shutter is employed to filter the focal plane spectrum, then a retransformation of the filtered spectrum by a second lens would regenerate the A4 page with only those characters of a specified type present. By cycling through the corresponding shutter patterns, the positions of all the characters could be found. Such a process would require a large detector array in addition to a fast, programmable spatial filter of high resolution.

Although the filter does not exist, there are materials that will record light patterns with high resolution. Since these materials respond to the time-averaged intensity of the light wave, the phase information is lost unless a reference wavefront is introduced to interfere with the light pattern. This is the technique of **holography**, the development of which is detailed in the next section. The pioneer of holography, Gabor, described a scheme for holographic character recognition in which the reference wavefront for each character differed [20]. When the hologram is illuminated from the page, a different code is generated by each character, and the code patterns are designed for unambiguous recognition by a computer. A more modern technique, by Merkle, which will be described later, uses a uniform wavefront for holographic recording, but the recognition is assisted by microcomputer analysis of the light distribution at the detection plane.

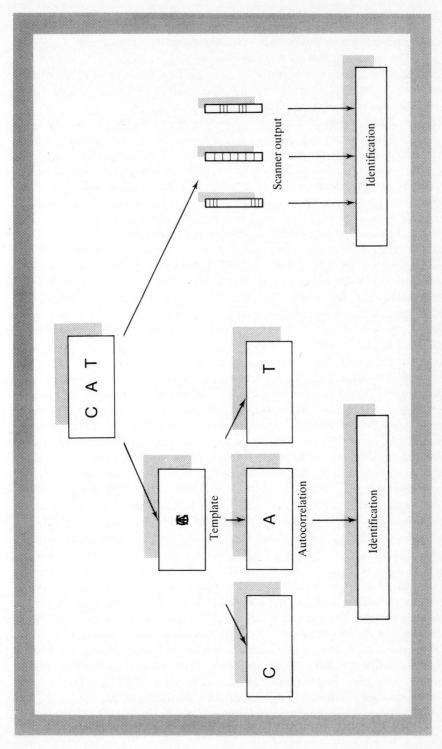

Figure 1.3 Document reader.

1.4   Historical introduction to holography

The idea of holography was introduced to the scientific community by Gabor in 1948 [21]. It arose from his work to improve the resolution of the conventional electron microscope beyond 5 Å. The electron beam has a de Broglie wavelength of 0.05 Å, but the viewing optics (electron lenses) reduce the resolution, due to aberrations. Therefore, Gabor suggested that the image be recorded and then inspected at visible wavelengths, where the viewing optics is corrected for aberrations to a high degree. When the electron beam that is diffracted by the object interferes with the undiffracted beam in the recording process, a recording can be formed, from which a complete reconstruction of the object is possible during viewing. The recording, or **hologram**, is then interrogated by a light beam which is a replica of the undiffracted electron beam, properly scaled according to the wavelength ratio.

Gabor verified experimentally the principle that an image of an object could be recorded at one wavelength and reconstructed at a second wavelength, using visible light in both cases [21]. Two important developments have followed this invention. In the first place, when the recording is made using visible light, the distance between the object and reference beams can be increased without exceeding the resolution limitations of the recording medium (provided that the coherence length of the light source exceeds the difference in path lengths of the two beams) (Figure 1.4(b)). This off-axis method of recording, which was suggested in 1962 [22], offers the advantage of spatially separating the beams that are generated when the hologram is reconstructed. There are three of these, of which one is the beam of interest, so that spatial separation is important for noise reduction (Figure 1.5). A second development was the recording of Fourier holograms, rather than Fresnel holograms. The geometrical shadow of an object will persist up to a large distance if there is a large disparity between the size of the structures that compose the object and the wavelength of light. Eventually, at infinity, the shadow will have decomposed into a spatial frequency spectrum of the object. This can be facilitated by a lens, which brings the frequency plane from infinity to the focal plane of the lens. The Fourier hologram is typically formed by interfering the focal plane spectrum with a plane wave, and is a higher resolution recording than the Fresnel hologram, which uses the geometrical shadow (Figure 1.4). (Alternatively, the object wave can be interfered with a reference wave that issues from a pinhole at the same distance from the recording plane as the object.) It is of higher resolution in the following respect. The Fresnel hologram is limited in resolution due to the granularity of the recording medium. However, since the Fourier transform is a transformation from the spatial domain to the frequency domain, the higher resolution structure will be represented by points that are more distant from the optic axis than the lower resolution structure. Therefore, the sole limitation on the resolution is the size of the recording medium.

The Fourier hologram was an important development in the history of holography because it allowed us to think of the high resolutions that were

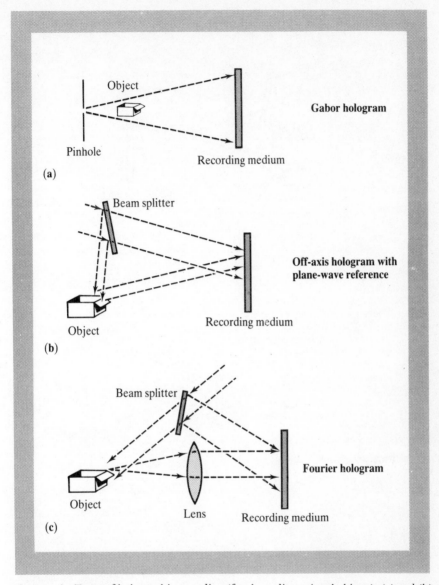

Figure 1.4   Types of holographic recording (for three-dimensional objects). (a) and (b) are also classified as Fresnel (or shadow) holograms.

the original motivation for the study of this subject. In our more restricted domain of interest, it is important for another reason. It is the only type of hologram where the hologram plane is flat rather than corrugated. The shadow of an object differs from an exact replica due to the structure that radiates spherical wavefronts. The higher resolution structure radiates wavefronts of high angular aperture, so that the shadow of fine points on the

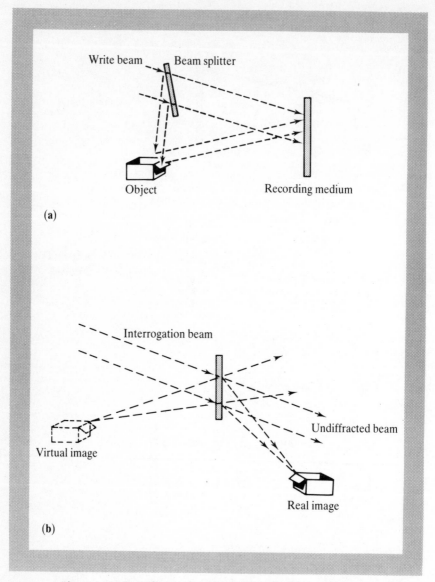

Figure 1.5   Recording and reconstruction of off-axis holograms.

object develops haloes around these points at a short distance from the object. This is evidence of the quadratic phase curvature that is recorded on the Fresnel hologram. It is preferable, in our application, to have a 'flat phase' recording because the overall phase of the recording is important for the shift invariance of the recognition process. The Fourier transform is a shift invariant transform. The location of the object in the field of view can be retrieved from the overall phase of the recording when an off-axis method is used. However, shadow holograms are not shift invariant and they are less suitable for the pattern recognition machines for that reason. Nonetheless, if the exact location of the object is known, the shadow hologram could offer an alternative recording strategy where the dynamic range of the recording is less than the Fourier hologram. This is important when the dynamic range of the recording medium is limited, but it has not been exploited in practice. Moreover, the spatial invariance of the conventional (Fourier) optical correlator is more limited in practice than is generally appreciated. This is due to the common usage of thick recording materials and the restrictions these impose on Bragg matching (Section 4.3). However, in the Fresnel situation, the diffraction efficiency of the hologram is not influenced by the lateral extent of the object.

It is important that the two beams that interfere to form the hologram are coherent and remain coherent for the duration of the recording. This has limited the usefulness of these systems in the past, because the only light sources were incandescent, and, consequently, of low efficiency. However, the advent of the laser has opened up the following areas for exploitation:

- interferometry for vibration and stress analysis, thermal deformation, composite inspection;
- fabrication of holographic optical elements for beam scanning, optical testing and display;
- particle sizing;
- high-resolution photolithography; and
- microscopy for analysis of tracks in high-energy physics experiments.

CHAPTER 2
MATHEMATICAL PRELIMINARIES

2.1 Introduction

The main purpose of this chapter is to provide an understanding of how the lens provides a spatial Fourier transform of an image. The result of this transform is a two-dimensional spatial frequency spectrum of the image, so that an understanding of spatial frequency is a prime requisite. An explanation of this is followed by a brief resume of the results of scalar diffraction theory. This theory explains how the intensity and phase distribution in an image evolves as the image-bearing light beam propagates through the optical system. There follows a mathematical description of lens focussing, culminating with Section 2.5, where the preceding results are combined to account for the Fourier transform property. Some relevant properties of the transform are reviewed in Section 2.6, followed by a mathematical description of correlation.

2.2 Spatial frequency

The electric field of a light wave, at one instant of time, is described by the following exponential function:

$$E(x, y, z) = E_o\, e^{-2\pi i (ux+vy+wz)}$$

The components u, v and w obey the following equation:

$$u^2 + v^2 + w^2 = \frac{n^2}{\lambda^2} = \frac{k^2}{\cdot 4\pi^2}$$

where n is the refractive index of the medium through which the light wave propagates, λ is the vacuum wavelength and k is the **wave vector** of the light wave.

Due to the small magnitude of λ, the spatial variation is not readily observed, except in the phenomena of interference and diffraction. For example, if a beam of light is divided equally into two beams by a beam splitter, and the beams are subsequently recombined with a small angle of intersection, then interference fringes will be formed perpendicular to the plane containing the intersecting beams. The two waves are represented by:

$$E_1 = \left(\frac{E_o}{2}\right) \exp\left[\frac{2\pi i}{\lambda}(x \sin\theta + z \cos\theta)\right]$$

$$E_2 = \left(\frac{E_o}{2}\right) \exp\left[\frac{2\pi i}{\lambda}(-x \sin\theta + z \cos\theta)\right]$$

where 2θ is the angle of intersection (Figure 2.1). The intensity of the interference pattern is given by:

$$|E_1 + E_2|^2 = E_o^2 \cos^2\left(\frac{2\pi\theta x}{\lambda}\right) \qquad \sin\theta \simeq \theta$$

The intensity maxima extend in the y-direction and are observed as a grating. The repetition period of grating is λ/θ, and its inverse is the spatial frequency of the grating. The units for the grating spatial frequency are mm^{-1} or line pairs/mm (lp/mm).

2.3   Scalar diffraction theory

Apertures and gratings of high spatial frequency diffract an incident light beam. The mathematics of the diffraction is described by the Rayleigh–Sommerfeld diffraction formula [4]. This integral gives the amplitude of the electric field at a point behind the grating, $E(\mathbf{r}')$, in terms of the amplitude of the electric field at points on the grating, $E(\mathbf{r})$:

$$E(\mathbf{r}') = \frac{i}{\lambda} \int_s E(\mathbf{r})\, \frac{e^{ikR}}{R} \cos\left[\theta(\mathbf{r})\right] ds$$

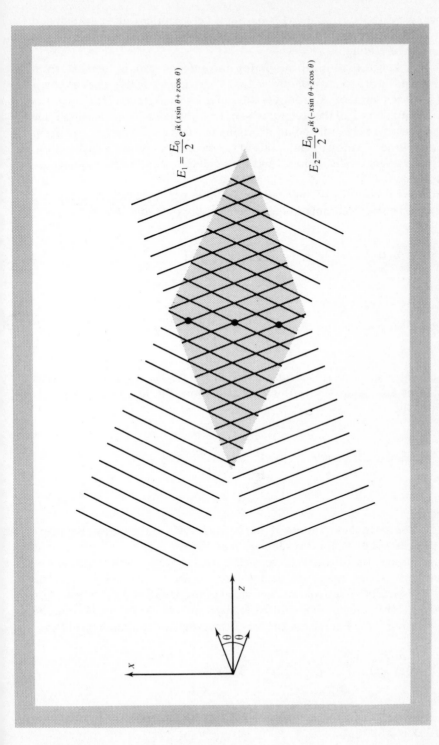

$$E_1 = \frac{E_0}{2} e^{jk(x\sin\theta + z\cos\theta)}$$

$$E_2 = \frac{E_0}{2} e^{jk(-x\sin\theta + z\cos\theta)}$$

Figure 2.1 Interference of two plane waves.

where $R = |\mathbf{r}' - \mathbf{r}|$, and $\theta(\mathbf{r})$ is the angle between the grating normal and $(\mathbf{r}' - \mathbf{r})$ (Figure 2.2). The integration is performed over the area of the aperture or grating.

A conceptual justification for the integral can be derived from Huyghens theory of secondary wavelets. The mathematical form of a spherical wave at a distance, R, from a point source is $(\exp ikR)/\lambda R$. The integral is the summation of all the secondary wavelets, giving each one the amplitude of the electric field at its point of origin. The inclination factor, $\cos [\theta(\mathbf{r})]$, describes the variation of amplitude of the secondary wavelet with direction. This is conventionally omitted, and the small errors due to its exclusion are calculated in [23].

In the majority of applications of this integral, the exponential phase factor is treated according to the paraxial approximation; that is:

$$R = [(z' - z)^2 + (x' - x)^2 + (y' - y)^2]^{1/2}$$

$$\simeq (z' - z) + \frac{(x' - x)^2 + (y' - y)^2}{2(z' - z)}$$

$$\simeq (z' - z) - \frac{x'x + y'y}{(z' - z)}$$

where the z-axis is perpendicular to the diffracting screen and the off-axis distances are small. Under this approximation, the Kirchhoff integral is written as:

$$E(\mathbf{r}') = \frac{ie^{ikz_o}}{\lambda z_o} \iint E(\mathbf{r}) \ \exp\left[-\frac{ik(x'x + y'y)}{z_o}\right] dx \, dy$$

where $z_o = z' - z$.

The diffraction pattern in the far-field, where the paraxial approximation is valid, is the two-dimensional Fourier transform of the light distribution at the diffracting screen. The frequency variables of the Fourier transform are the spatial frequency components, $x'/\lambda z_o$ and $y'/\lambda z_o$. The spatial frequency spectrum of the screen is displayed in the far-field. For example, when a light beam is diffracted by a pinhole, the far-field amplitude distribution is the Fourier transform of the cylinder function defined by:

$$E(\mathbf{r}) = 1, \quad r \le a; \qquad E(\mathbf{r}) = 0, \quad r > a$$

The Fourier transform is an Airy disk and rings (Figure 2.3), and the radius of the disk is $0.61 \, \lambda z_o/a$.

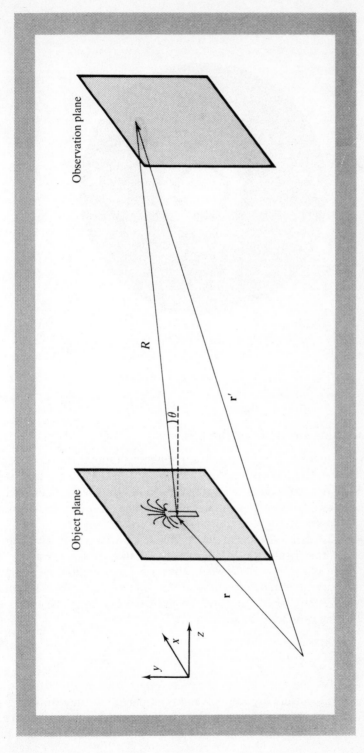

Figure 2.2 Co-ordinate system for variables in the Rayleigh–Sommerfeld diffraction integral.

Figure 2.3   The Airy pattern.

2.4   Focussing property of the lens

A convex lens focusses a collimated beam of light to a spot in the focal plane. If the collimated beam propagates parallel to the optic axis of the lens, then the spot is on this axis and is called the **focal point** (or **focus**). Geometrical considerations lead to an exponential function which expresses the focussing action, as follows.

Figure 2.4 demonstrates the focussing of an off-axis ray by a plano-convex lens. The optical path difference between this off-axis ray and a ray along the optic axis is $(1 - n)\,\delta t$, where n is the refractive index of the glass. From elementary circle geometry, $\delta t \simeq \rho^2/2R$. Moreover, the focal length of the lens is $f = R/(n - 1)$. Therefore, the phase retardance can be expressed by the following exponential function:

$$\exp\left(-\frac{ik\rho^2}{2f}\right)$$

The off-axis ray suffers a phase advance compared with the on-axis ray. Therefore, the wavefront leaves the lens as a circular arc (whose centre is the focus of the lens). The geometrical approximations that enter into this

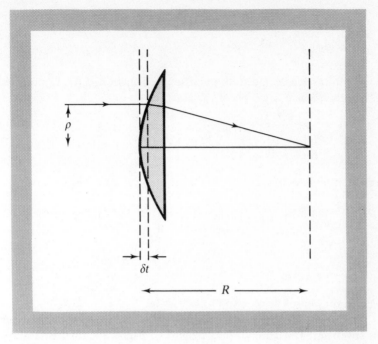

Figure 2.4   The refraction of a ray of light by a plano-convex lens.

derivation can be included to give the departure of this wavefront from a circle arc and the consequent effect on the focussed spot size [24]. In the case of a symmetrical biconvex lens, the optical path difference is $2(1 - n)\,\delta t$ and the focal length is $f = R/[2(n - 1)]$. Therefore, the phase retardance is expressed by the same exponential function.

2.5   Fourier transform property of the lens

We have shown (Section 2.3) that the diffraction pattern in the far-field is a Fourier transform of the aperture function at the diffracting screen. The insertion of a lens at the diffracting screen produces a demagnified image of the far-field distribution in the focal plane of the lens. This can be shown using the results of Sections 2.3 and 2.4:

$$E(\mathbf{r}') = \frac{i}{\lambda} \int_{s} E(\mathbf{r})\ \frac{e^{ikR}}{R}\ ds$$

where:

$$R \simeq z_o + \frac{(x' - x)^2 + (y' - y)^2}{2z_o}$$

and:

$$ds = dx\, dy$$

When the lens is inserted, the aperture function, $E(\mathbf{r})$, is modified by the phase retardance function of the lens:

$$E(\mathbf{r}) \rightarrow E(\mathbf{r})\ \exp\left[-\frac{ik\,(x^2 + y^2)}{2f}\right]$$

Therefore, in the focal plane ($z_o = f$), the integral is simplified, and:

$$E(x', y') = \frac{i}{\lambda f}\ \exp\left[\frac{ik(x'^2 + y'^2)}{2f}\right] \iint E(x, y)$$

$$\exp\left[-\frac{ik\,(x'x + y'y)}{f}\right] dx\, dy$$

(The constant phase factor, $\exp(-ikz_o)$, is ignored.)

The intensity distribution in the focal plane is the spatial frequency power spectrum. The demagnification with respect to the far-field is the ratio of the focal length to far-field distance. The physical area of the spectrum is usually much smaller than the area of the diffracting screen because the pattern on the screen is usually coarse by comparison with the wavelength of light. This produces diffraction at small field angles with the result that the spectrum is close to the optic axis. It is the reciprocal of the feature size on the screen, multiplied by λf, which gives a metric to the focal plane.

When the diffracting screen is located in the front focal plane of the lens, an exact Fourier transform relationship exists between the front and back focal plane; that is, the quadratic phase factor is removed. This is demonstrated mathematically using different approaches in [4] and [25]. The phase delay that each spatial frequency component experiences, in propagation from the screen to the lens, cancels this quadratic phase term [4].

The diffraction integral was applied to lens focussing in the previous section to demonstrate the Fourier transform property, the propagation from the lens to the focus being represented by a single integral. However, when the diffracting screen is placed in the front focal plane of the lens, two integrals are required; and in a correlator system, where two Fourier transformations are performed, four integrals are required. To eliminate the cumbersome mathematics involved in such systems, an operator notation was formulated [26]. The phase factors, which are quadratic in the spatial coordinates, are written in a condensed form and their mathematical properties are tabulated. The conditions required for the cancellation of these phase factors in the diffraction integral can then be rapidly assessed. This technique has been extended to finite aperture systems in [27], and is of particular importance when the lens aperture is comparable with the area of the diffracting screen. However, as the Fourier transform is not exact, due to the attenuation of the higher spatial frequencies, a generous requirement on the lens diameter is needed to avoid this: the lens diameter must be twice the diameter of the diffracting screen [23]. (This technique has not been extended to the treatment of optical aberrations because these are not spatially invariant.)

2.6   Some properties of the Fourier transform

The forward and inverse one-dimensional Fourier transforms are defined by:

$$F[g(x)] = G(u) = \int g(x)\ e^{-2\pi iux}\ dx$$

$$F^{-1}[G(u)] = g(x) = \int G(u)\ e^{2\pi iux}\ du$$

(Integral limits in this and the following section run from $-\infty$ to $+\infty$.) The following corollaries follow from these definitions:

(1)   A symmetric function has a symmetric Fourier transform, which is real if the function is real.

(2)   An anti-symmetric function has an anti-symmetric Fourier transform, which is imaginary if the function is real.

(3)   The lens performs forward Fourier transforms, exclusively.

(4)   The Fourier shift theorem:

$$\int g(x + x_o)\ e^{-2\pi iux}\ dx = e^{2\pi iux_o}\ G(u)$$

(5)   The similarity theorem:

$$F[g(ax)] = |a|^{-1}\ G\left(\frac{u}{a}\right)$$

(6)   The convolution theorem (see later):

$$F[g \otimes h] = G(u)\ H(u)$$

where $g \otimes h = \int g(x)\ h(\chi - x)\ dx$

(7)   Two forward Fourier transforms return the original image, but with inverted co-ordinate axis:

$$F[g(x)] = F^{-1}[g(-x)]$$

$$\therefore \quad FF[g(x)] = g(-x)$$

A lens will perform an exact Fourier transform of an image that is centred on the optic axis. However, if the image is laterally translated, then the Fourier shift theorem shows that the Fourier transform will be multiplied by a phase factor. Chapter 3 will explain how the position of the image is recovered from this phase term in the optical correlator. The similarity theorem shows that a scaling of the image produces a scaled Fourier transform, which the conventional optical correlator fails to recognize.

The convolution theorem is frequently used in Fourier optics; for example, when the image plane light distribution can be expressed as the product of two or more functions for which the Fourier transforms are known. Lists of Fourier transforms of basic functions are given in, for example, [28], and three relevant ones are illustrated in Figure 2.5. When the image is written on a pixellated input device (see Section 4.5.1 for examples), the image is initially sampled:

$$f_s(x, y) = f_o(x, y) \, \text{comb}\left(\frac{x}{p_x}\right) \text{comb}\left(\frac{y}{p_y}\right)$$

where $f_s(x, y)$ is the sampled image, $f_o(x, y)$ is the original image, p_x is the repeat spacing of the pixels in the x-direction and p_y is the repeat spacing of the pixels in the y-direction.

Then the sampled points are extended in the x- and y-directions according to the pixel dimensions:

$$f_{sp}(x, y) = f_x(x, y) \otimes \left[\text{rect}\left(\frac{x}{\Delta a_x}\right) \text{rect}\left(\frac{y}{\Delta a_y}\right) \right]$$

where $f_{sp}(x, y)$ is the sampled image on the pixel array, Δa_x is the pixel width in the x-direction and Δa_y is the pixel width in the y-direction.

Finally, the limited extent of the array is accounted for:

$$f_{dev}(x, y) = f_{sp}(x, y) \, \text{rect}\left(\frac{x}{w_x}\right) \text{rect}\left(\frac{y}{w_y}\right)$$

where $f_{dev}(x, y)$ is the image that appears on the device, w_x is the width of the array in the x-direction and w_y is the width of the array in the y-direction.

2.7   Correlation

The one-dimensional autocorrelation and cross-correlation integrals are defined by:

$$g^* \odot g = \int g^*(x - \chi) \, g(x) \, dx$$

$$g^* \odot h = \int g^*(x - \chi) \, h(x) \, dx$$

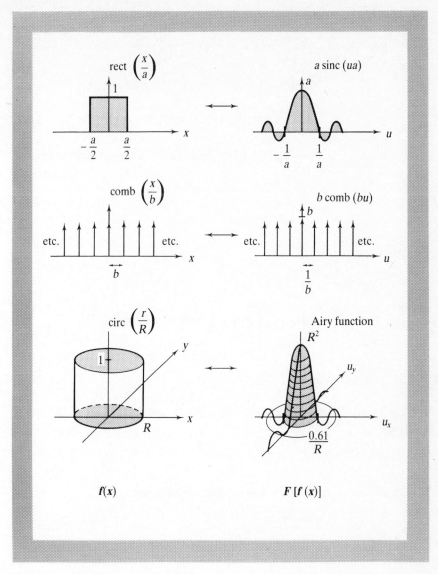

Figure 2.5 Some useful functions and their Fourier transforms.

The cross-correlation and convolution integrals can be generated, optically, by forward Fourier transforms of products of the frequency spectra of $g(x)$ and $h(x)$. For example:

$$F[G*H] = -g* \odot h$$
$$F^{-1}[GH] = g \otimes h$$

This can be demonstrated mathematically, as follows:

$$F[g^* \odot h] = \int \left[\int g^*(x)\ h(x - \chi)\ dx \right] e^{-2\pi i u \chi}\ d\chi$$

$$= \int g^*(x) \left[\int h(x - \chi)\ e^{-2\pi i u \chi}\ d\chi \right] dx$$

$$= - \int g^*(x) \left[\int h(\chi' + x)\ e^{-2\pi i u \chi'}\ d\chi' \right] dx$$

$$= - \int g^*(x)\ e^{2\pi i u x}\ H(u)\ dx \qquad \text{(Fourier shift theorem)}$$

$$= - \left[\int g(x)\ e^{-iux}\ dx \right] * H(u)$$

$$= - G^*(u)\ H(u)$$

Similarly:

$$F^{-1}[g \otimes h] = \int \left[\int g(x)\ h(\chi - x)\ dx \right] e^{2\pi i u \chi}\ d\chi$$

$$= \int g(x) \left[\int h(\chi - x)\ e^{2\pi i u \chi}\ d\chi \right] dx$$

$$= \int g(x)\ e^{-2\pi i u x}\ H(u)\ dx \qquad \text{(Fourier shift theorem)}$$

$$= G(u)\ H(u)$$

An important result links the autocorrelation function with the power spectrum:

$$g \odot g = F^{-1}[G^*G]$$

This result is known as the **Wiener–Khinchine theorem**.

CHAPTER 3
DESIGN OF THE OPTICAL SYSTEM

3.1 Introduction

This chapter first discusses the distinction between incoherent and coherent processing systems and then is devoted to the topic of coherent processing. Two generic types of coherent correlator are presented. As the main difference between these is the manner in which the Fourier plane processing is performed, the description of each system is followed by an analysis of the Fourier plane processing. Sections 3.5 and 3.6 provide the analysis that underpins the selection of the laser and the Fourier transform lens in these systems. The physical dimensions of practical systems are discussed in the final section.

3.2 Incoherent and coherent systems

The temporal coherence of a light beam is determined by the monochromaticity of the light source, and its spatial coherence by the beam expansion system. Lasers and filtered arc discharge lamps are examples of sources with a high degree of temporal coherence, while white light sources and LEDs (light-emitting diodes) are treated as temporally incoherent for practical purposes.

Systems that can be realized with incoherent light sources are fundamentally different from those that are coherent. The Fourier transform relationship does not exist for the incoherent case, and so correlation cannot be achieved by this means. An example of a particular type of incoherent correlator is shown in Figure 3.1 [29]. The diffuse light source at the focal plane of the first lens generates a spread of beams with various angles with respect to the optic axis. One beam is shown, and the intensity of its image point is the product of the transmission of the object transparency and a displaced template transparency. The overlap of the two transparencies at different degrees of displacement is represented by separate image point intensities, so that the intensity distribution on the screen is the direct correlation of the template and object intensities. A mathematical analysis of this and other systems is presented in [30].

The coherent systems perform correlation according to one principle; namely, the multiplication of the Fourier transforms of object and template amplitude/phase distributions and the subsequent Fourier transformation of the product. When the input is in the form of a transparency, an amplitude distribution is implied. However, with some types of refresh input devices the input images are represented by phase distributions (see Chapter 4). In one type of system, a hologram is produced by interfering one of the Fourier transforms with a reference beam. The subsequent interrogation of this hologram by the second Fourier transform yields the product (Section 3.3). In the second type of system, the Fourier transforms are interfered directly and interrogation by a reference beam yields the product (Section 3.4).

Although the incoherent systems require input devices of lower optical quality than coherent systems, with significant cost advantages, the processing power is more limited. The number of data points that can be processed by this method is about 10^4 [30], compared with about 10^6 for a coherent system. This limitation is imposed by diffraction at the input device. Incoherent systems depend on the rectilinear propagation of light, and this will only pertain to a relatively coarse mesh of data points. In contrast, the Fourier transform in coherent systems is generated by diffraction, and the development of higher resolution input devices enhances the diffractive effect. A further limitation on processing power is the inability to represent negative numbers in an intensity distribution, whereas they are handled naturally in an amplitude/phase representation. Nonetheless, some work continues on the incoherent systems, particularly on exploiting the wavelength coding of information, and a summary is contained in [31].

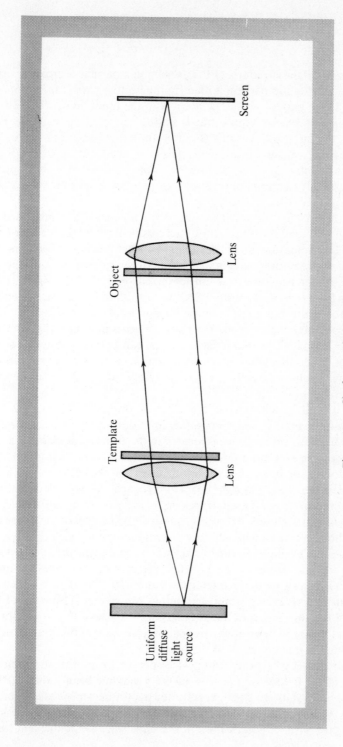

Figure 3.1 Shadow casting correlator.

3.3   The correlator with memory

3.3.1   Description

In the **frequency plane correlator (FPC)**, the input pattern is compared with a fixed template. This comparison is made in the Fourier plane for the following reason. If the pattern is moved laterally in the input plane, the Fourier spectrum remains fixed in space but is multiplied by a phase factor that depends on the lateral movement (Fourier shift theorem). Therefore, the pattern matching can proceed independently of the location of the input pattern. The template itself is recorded as a hologram – that is, both phase and amplitude information are recorded. Consequently, the location of the input pattern is recorded in the hologram.

One method for the construction of the hologram was proposed by Vander Lugt [32], and the correlator based on this is called the **Vander Lugt correlator**. The hologram is called a **matched filter** because it contains the complex conjugate of the frequency spectrum of the pattern. In communication theory, a matched filter is a time-reversed version of the signal, and, when such a filter is used, the output SNR is maximized for the case when the input noise is white noise. In the present application, the matched filter approach is valuable because the filter can be generated optically, and the output beam from the filter is a plane wave that can be focussed to give a correlation spot. Its disadvantage is that small changes in the scale or rotation of the object will prohibit detection, unless more powerful techniques are used (see Chapter 7).

The optical generation of the filter is shown in Figure 3.2. An expanded laser beam is incident upon the input device, which is a reflective one in this case. The input device is located in the front focal plane of a lens and a holographic recording device is placed in the back focal plane. The devices are located orthogonal to the optic axis so that the Fourier spectrum is in focus across the plate. The light beam interrogates the input device orthogonally by preference, as the interfaces on the device can be anti-reflection coated in a standard manner. However, quasi-normal angles of incidence can be used without prejudice when desired to avoid the second pass through the beam splitter; for example, in those cases when beam intensity is important. The amplitude and phase of the Fourier spectrum are recorded by interference with a plane wave derived from the same laser. The angle between the **object beam** and **reference beam** determines the spatial frequency of the interference fringes (Section 2.2). It is advisable to have this angle appreciable so that there will be an adequate spatial separation of the reconstructed beams during the interrogation of the hologram.

In those cases where the input device operates by rotating the polarization vector of the light wave (Section 4.2), a **polarizing beam splitter (PBS)** replaces the beam splitter. The light reflected off the device holds a polarization image, which is converted to an amplitude image by the PBS. The light that is reflected with its polarization in the same state as the incident beam

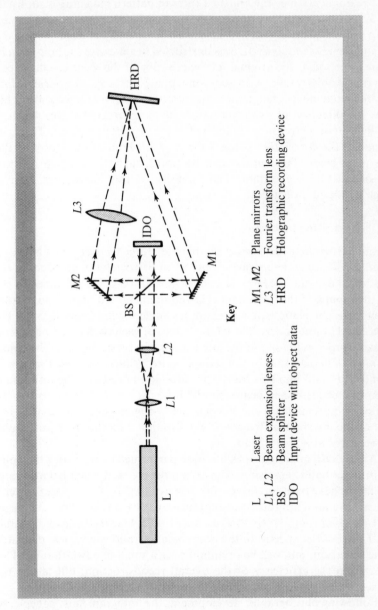

Figure 3.2 The fabrication of a matched filter.

Key

L	Laser	M1, M2	Plane mirrors
L1, L2	Beam expansion lenses	L3	Fourier transform lens
BS	Beam splitter	HRD	Holographic recording device
IDO	Input device with object data		

passes straight through the PBS. Although the image contrast is imposed by the PBS, it is actually the input device that is located in the front focal plane of the lens.

The application of the matched filter to pattern matching is shown in Figure 3.3. The scene data formed on the input device is Fourier transformed and superposed precisely on the hologram of the object data. When the object and scene are equivalent, a **reconstructed beam** leaves the hologram in the same direction as the original reference beam. If the scene is a displaced version of the object, there is an additional phase factor in the Fourier transform which increments the spatial frequency of the reconstructed wave. This changes the direction of propagation of the reconstructed wave, which is sensed by a photodetector array located in the correlation plane. The light amplitude in the correlation plane is the forward Fourier transform of the reconstructed beam. This was shown in Section 2.7 to be the cross-correlation of the object and scene data. The intensity of this cross-correlation is recorded by the photodetector.

3.3.2   Fourier plane processing

When the hologram is reconstructed, there are three reconstructed beams in all (Figure 3.4). Each beam gives some form of correlation product in the correlation plane, and the lateral extent of each of these is determined by the size of the input and the scene data. The requirement that there is no overlap between these correlations sets a minimum angle for the intersection of the reference and object beams. The lateral extent of each correlation product is of the same order as the size of the input scene, if it is assumed that the object size is much less than that of the scene (Figure 3.5(a)). Suppose that this is 2 cm and an $F/4$ 40 mm lens forms the correlation product. Then, the angle between the reconstructed beams should be $\Theta = \frac{1}{8}$ or $7°$. This also sets the resolution requirement on the Fourier plane device, since the spatial frequency of the interference fringes is Θ/λ (Section 2.2); that is, 5 μm resolution is required at $\lambda = 0.63$ μm.

All the system design work has been performed by recording the hologram on silver halide emulsion. The exposure level and beam balance ratio requirements have been extensively investigated in [33]. The exposure level is chosen to give an amplitude transmittance of between 50–70%. The beam balance ratio, or $|R|^2/|O|^2$, is chosen as 1 or 2. Due to the large dynamic range of the Fourier spectrum, the beam balance ratio will vary appreciably over the spectrum, and will be optimum over a small bandwidth only. This detracts from the efficiency of the overall reconstruction, but allows the emphasis of the spatial frequency range pertinent to a specified object.

Following photographic development, the hologram must be replaced in its original position. This requires a three-axis fine adjustment facility on the hologram mount. An adjustment sensitivity of a few microns perpendicular to the optic axis and a few tens of microns along the optic axis would

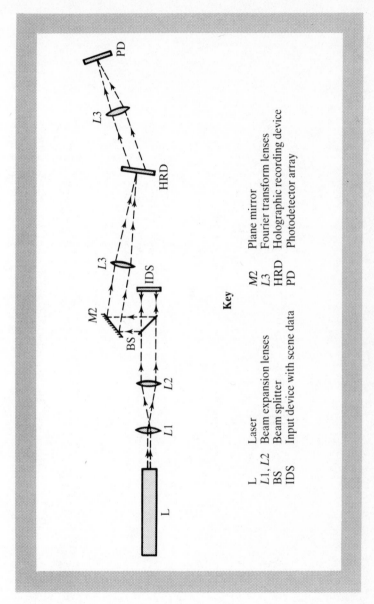

Figure 3.3   The employment of a matched filter.

Key

L	Laser	M2	Plane mirror
L1, L2	Beam expansion lenses	L3	Fourier transform lenses
BS	Beam splitter	HRD	Holographic recording device
IDS	Input device with scene data	PD	Photodetector array

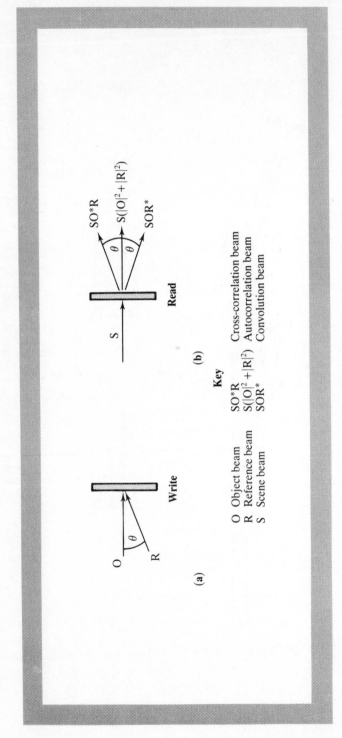

Figure 3.4 The reconstructed beams in a frequency plane correlator.

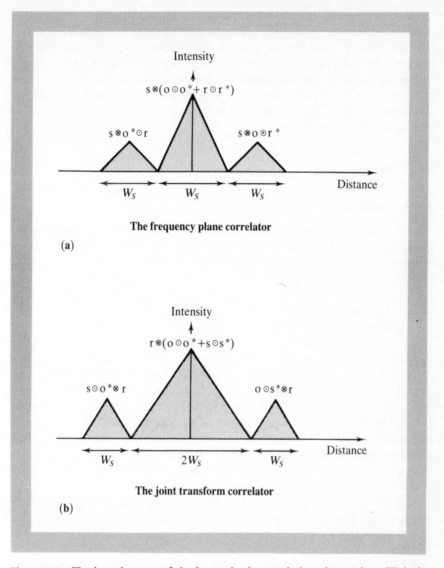

Figure 3.5   The lateral extent of the beams in the correlation plane (where W_o is the width of the object, W_s is the width of the scene and $W_o \ll W_s$).

be ideal for most cases [34], but can be relaxed for less demanding pattern recognition [35].

This detailed adjustment can be avoided by using a modern material for the recording of the hologram that does not require a development stage. Such materials are called **real-time holographic materials**, and will be discussed in Chapter 5.

Finally, there are the minor sources of degradation; that is, those that produce only small effects in this particular system. In the first place, the hologram thickness limits the region of the scene plane over which the object can be tracked. The system is then described as space variant. **Spatial variance** becomes more important for the thicker recording materials, and a fuller discussion is given in Chapter 5. Secondly, the optical aberrations of this form of matched filter in comparison with other forms of matched filter are calculated [36]. The only aberration is distortion in the correlation output for this system configuration.

3.4   The correlator with no memory

3.4.1   Description

In the **joint transform correlator (JTC)**, the object and scene patterns are presented at the input plane contemporaneously. Both are Fourier transformed and the interference pattern of their Fourier transforms recorded in the Fourier plane. The subsequent interrogation of this interference pattern with a collimated beam yields the correlation products of the object and the scene. The optical system is shown in its basic form in Figure 3.6.

This system was originally proposed as an improvement on the Vander Lugt correlator in those situations where there is considerable similarity between the object and the scene [37]. At about the same time as this proposal, it was pointed out that this system relaxes the precise positioning requirement of the memory correlator, a requirement that is more severe when large data inputs are considered [38]. The contemporary advantage of the system lies in its greater parallelism. Provided that the real-time devices are available, search routines can be performed at frame rates, rather than requiring two frames for each processing operation. However, this may cause a significant 'materials' problem to fabricate a fast holographic device with a memory for the Vander Lugt correlator.

The JTC, however, places more demands on the optical quality of the input device and the Fourier transforming lens. The device phase noise is cancelled in the memory correlator when the object is located in the scene in the same position as when the hologram was recorded. Therefore, the correlation output could, in principle, be optimized in this configuration by lateral motion of the scene or template. However, in the JTC, the object and scene information are placed on different input devices or separated areas of the same input device. Therefore, phase noise cancellation can never be complete.

3.4.2   Fourier plane processing

To achieve an adequate separation of the correlation products, the object and scene Fourier transforms must be brought together with a finite angle between their beams (Figure 3.7). Since this angle determines, in part, the

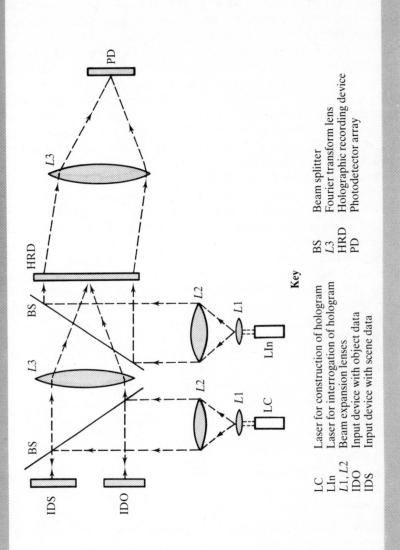

Key

LC	Laser for construction of hologram	BS	Beam splitter
LIn	Laser for interrogation of hologram	L3	Fourier transform lens
L1, L2	Beam expansion lenses	HRD	Holographic recording device
IDO	Input device with object data	PD	Photodetector array
IDS	Input device with scene data		

Figure 3.6 The joint transform correlator.

aperture of the Fourier transform lens, it is important to obtain some assessment of its magnitude. This can be done, conveniently, by comparison with the memory correlator. The on-axis term in the memory correlator is the cross-correlation of the scene with the autocorrelation of the object; in the JTC, it is the sum of the autocorrelation of the scene and the autocorrelation of the object. The correlation peak of interest, the cross-correlation of the object and scene, is the off-axis term and has the same size in each system. In general, the scene information is spatially more extensive than the object, so that the DC term in the JTC is twice the size of the DC term in the memory correlator (Figure 3.5(b)). Therefore, a higher resolution is required of the holographic recording material. In addition, a larger aperture Fourier transform lens is required. Alternatively, the input planes could be tilted and Fourier transformed on to a common point in the focal plane using two 2 cm lenses. However, the Fourier transform planes would not be coplanar and efficient interference would take place only in a limited spatial frequency band (see dual-axis correlator in Section 6.6).

A salient advantage of the JTC is that interference is arranged between two Fourier spectra rather than a Fourier spectrum and a plane wave. Because of the large dynamic range of Fourier spectra, it is not possible to match the amplitude with that of a plane wave over the complete spectral range. Consequently, fringes of large modulation depth occur only over a select band of frequencies in the memory correlator. However, there is a closer match of amplitudes over a broader frequency range when two Fourier spectra are interfered. The modulation depth of the fringe system will approach 100% when the object and scene are equivalent. Hence, more efficient diffraction of the interrogation beam is assured, although the possibility of simultaneous spatial frequency filtering in the focal plane is lost. In addition, the interrogation of the hologram with a plane wave rather than an image transform simplifies the reconstruction process.

Evidence for the high sensitivity of this correlator is given in [39]. An example of a hybrid digital/optical correlator for image processing is contained in [40].

3.5 The laser: Coherence and power requirements

3.5.1 Temporal coherence

The **temporal coherence** of the laser is the average duration of phase integrity of the light wave. This refers to the model of light as a series of wave trains where the average length of a train is the temporal coherence multiplied by the velocity of light. It is commonly expressed by the linewidth of the radiation, broad linewidths being associated with short temporal coherence. The mathematical connection is made via the Wiener–Khinchine theorem (Section 2.7). If the autocorrelation function of the light wave is a Gaussian

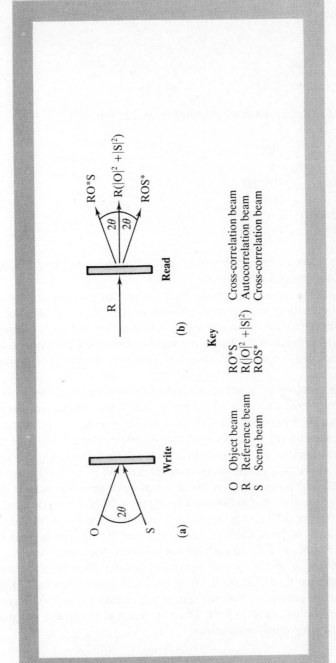

Figure 3.7   The reconstructed beams in a joint transform correlator.

function of time, then its spatial frequency power spectrum is also Gaussian, and the **half-height full widths (HHFW)** are inversely related. If the HHFW of the former is chosen as the **coherence length**, Δl, then:

$$\Delta l \, \Delta k = 1$$

$$\Delta l \sim \frac{\lambda^2}{\Delta \lambda}$$

The values for some typical multi-mode lasers are given by:

	$\dfrac{\Delta \lambda}{\lambda}$	Δl (cm)
HeNe	3×10^{-6}	18
Ar$^+$	10^{-5}	5
AlGaAs	2×10^{-3}	0.03
Nd:YAG	4×10^{-5}	0.25

(When these lasers are operated in single mode, the coherence length is ample for most holographic applications.)

There are two practical consequences of limited temporal coherence in the correlator. In the first place, the optical system design should be such that the path lengths between the two beams involved in forming the hologram do not exceed the coherence length. In the second place, both the Fourier spectrum and correlation peak may be blurred. These problems will be examined in turn.

In the memory correlator, the hologram is formed when the object transform interferes with a tilted reference wavefront. Therefore, the path difference between opposite sides of the Fourier spectrum is the minimum path difference that can be engineered in this system. For a 3 mm wide spectrum and a tilt angle of 7°, the path difference will be 3 sin 7°, which is about 0.4 mm. However, this minimum path difference will be difficult to achieve in practice because it assumes that the object and reference waves have equal paths through the system. On the other hand, the JTC places no demands on the temporal coherence in this respect. All rays between points in the front focal plane and the back focal plane (of the Fourier transform lens) have equal path lengths, so that no path length differences are incurred.

The blurring of the Fourier spectrum follows from the fact that λf determines the metric of the spectrum in the focal plane (Section 2.5). This blurring must be compared with the spot size in the focal plane to determine tolerable spectral bandwidths [35]. In order that the blurring is not distinguishable, the theoretical result gives:

$$\frac{\Delta \lambda}{\lambda} < \frac{1}{N}$$

where N is the number of pixels across the input device.

The practical limitation related to a specific recognition problem can be evaluated from the sensitivity of the recognition to scale changes on the input. This is an independent method of altering the scale of the Fourier transform. The tolerance can vary between 0.5% [33] and 8% [35], depending on the task. Then, $\Delta\lambda/\lambda$ takes the same value as the scaling tolerance.

The width of the correlation peak is the cross-correlation of the object and the scene. A high common spatial frequency will produce a narrow correlation peak. However, when the source has a finite linewidth, this must be compared with the resolution of the grating formed in the Fourier plane, to determine the effect on the correlation peak width [41]. When the grating can resolve this linewidth, the correlation peak will be broadened. The resolving power of a grating is the path difference between rays diffracted from opposite ends of the grating, in wavelengths. Therefore, the resolving power in the case of the parameters cited for the memory correlator is:

$$\frac{\lambda}{\Delta\lambda} = \frac{3 \times 10^3 \sin 7°}{0.63} = 800$$

for a Fourier plane recording of 3 mm width.

The resolving power of the JTC grating will be twice as large due to the larger angle of beam intersection. The maximum bandwidth is the reciprocal of the resolving power. These results were verified, practically, using a diode laser in [42].

3.5.2   Spatial coherence

The **spatial coherence** of an extended light beam refers to the lateral phase integrity across the wavefront. If the laser beam were expanded without employing a pinhole at the internal focus of the collimator, then the aberrations of the initial focussing lens might diminish the spatial coherence. The consequences of poor spatial coherence will be an attenuation in the amplitude of the spatial frequency spectrum, because efficient diffraction requires a fixed phase relationship across the width of the beam.

The choice of pinhole aperture and focal length of the collimating lens determine the diameter of the expanded beam, and the resolution that can be achieved in the Fourier spectrum. The laser beam is diffracted by the pinhole into a cone of semi-angle $0.61 \lambda/a$, where a is the radius of the pinhole. This cone contains 84% of the beam intensity, and the residue is contained in the Airy rings around this cone. It is convenient to arrange for the aperture of the collimating lens to encircle this central cone so that there is no diffraction from this aperture. If the collimating lens has a focal length f, then the diameter of the collimated beam will be $1.22 \lambda f/a$, and this will be equal to the aperture of the collimating lens. This beam has a flat phase wavefront, but the amplitude of the wavefront varies gradually from a central maximum to zero at the edges. If the input device covers the full wavefront, this will result in some degree of spatial variance (Section 5.3).

The spatial light distribution that falls on the Fourier transform lens is a product of the Airy function and the spatial information present on the input device. Therefore, the focal plane spectrum will be a convolution of the Fourier transforms of each of the factors. In particular, the spectral peaks will be broadened according to the spot size of the focussed beam. This spot size will be approximately equal to the pinhole aperture, multiplied by the ratio of the focal lengths of the Fourier transform and beam expansion lenses. This spot size affects the scale and rotational sensitivity of the pattern matching, since the larger the area of the spectral peaks, the less sensitive is the pattern matching to slight misalignments. It is also used to calculate the temporal coherence requirements in Section 3.5.1. The maximum pinhole size is such that the expanded beam fills the input device.

In the correlator described in the appendix, spatial filtering was not included in the beam expansion system in the interest of building a compact system. In this case, the spot size is the diameter of the laser beam waist at the beam expander, multiplied by the same ratio of focal lengths.

3.5.3 Power requirements

The laser dissipates the largest fraction of the electrical power required to operate the correlator. Since one of the salient advantages of the optical correlator, in comparison with its electronic counterpart, is the (much) lower power dissipation, it is important to minimize this parameter to gain the maximum advantage. In addition, lower laser powers are usually associated with smaller lasers. The FPC has seen more system development because the hologram can be generated in the laboratory and a laser diode can be used for interrogating it in the practical system. In contrast, the JTC typically requires an Argon laser in the system to write the holograms.

A benchmark for writing power requirements is the undergraduate experiment where a simple display hologram is made on silver halide emulsion using a helium neon laser of a few milliwatts output power. An exposure time of about one second is typical for such holograms and there are no vibration problems when an optical bench is employed. When Fourier plane holograms are considered, there is a considerable concentration of light at the hologram plane, so that improved efficiency might be expected. However, the light intensity at the spectral islands is much less than that in the central spot of the Fourier spectrum. In addition, all known real-time holographic materials are less sensitive than silver halide emulsion (see Table 5.1). For example, in the correlator of the appendix, a few milliwatts of argon laser power are required to saturate the hologram formed in the bismuth silicon oxide (BSO) in a few seconds; notwithstanding the absence of spatial filtering. Therefore, it is advisable to use 10–100 mW lasers for developmental work.

The power required for interrogating the hologram depends on the diffraction efficiency of the hologram (Section 5.3). In the case of BSO, this is a few percent, so that, although the camera in the correlation plane is considerably more sensitive than the BSO, a similar intensity of light is required for the read beam as for the write beam. A power of about 10 mW or higher is important in this case.

3.6   Design of the Fourier transform lens

The accuracy of the Fourier transform depends both on the precision with which the input and Fourier plane recording devices can be located, and the freedom from aberration of the lens systems. The fractional error of location is reduced if a long focal length lens is chosen. This is also consonant with aberration reduction. To reduce the overall length of the correlator, a telephoto requirement can be incorporated into the design specification of the lens system. A four-element lens system is detailed in [43], which has an equivalent focal length of 1 m, an overall length between focal planes of 1.4 m, and the aberrations are nowhere greater than $\lambda/8$. The effect of moving the input device along the optic axis can be calculated from the Kirchhoff integral. The Fourier transform is multiplied by a defocussing term, J_{def}, where:

$$J_{def} = \exp\left\{ -i\left[\frac{k\delta\,(x^2 + y^2)}{2f^2} \right] \right\}$$

Here, δ is the distance of defocus and x, y are the input plane co-ordinates.

The wavefront distortion in the exponential factor remains below $\lambda/8$ for a defocus, when the area of the input device is 1 cm^2 and the lens has a focal length of 1 m.

To take full advantage of the precision of the four-element system, the input and Fourier plane devices should have an optical quality better than $\lambda/8$, and the spatial frequency resolution of the input device should extend to 47 lp/mm. If these standards of tolerance are relaxed, as would be the case with a practical input device (see Table 4.1), then a simpler lens system can be employed. An experimental investigation of a particular telescope objective in [44] has shown that the wavefront error up to 40 lp/mm in a 35 mm input aperture is less than $\lambda/10$ (r.m.s.: root mean square). In the practical experience of the author, a high quality achromatic doublet can be used with spatial light modulators, whose aperture is about one-quarter that of the lens, and which have an optical quality less than a wavelength across the aperture. However, when such lenses are used, the Fourier transform can be obtained with lower aberration if the input device is placed adjacent to the lens rather than in the front focal plane [54b]. A general treatment of doublets can be found in [54c]. Where unequal focal length lenses are required for the two Fourier transforms in a correlator, a triplet design is more appropriate and one is given in [54d].

In those situations where the size of the correlator is more critical than the accuracy and amplitude efficiency of the Fourier transform, holographic lenses can be employed. These can be configured for reflection focussing and can also be incorporated into the matched filter.

The production of holographic lenses, for this application, is detailed in [45]. The design is facilitated by a ray-tracing program, and the practical results are compared with theory. The holographic lens concept is not favourable to multi-element systems because of the alignment problem and the reduced amplitude efficiency. Therefore, aberration reduction is limited. Fortunately, when the correlation peak SNR is adopted as a design criterion rather than the accuracy of the Fourier transform, the system is more tolerant to phase aberrations. The fabrication of a better holographic lens with modest equipment is described in [46].

The incorporation of the second Fourier transform lens into the matched filter is accomplished by using a point source as the reference beam. The position of the point source subsequently becomes the position of the unshifted correlation peak when the hologram is interrogated. The analysis of such 'lens-less matched filters' is contained in [36], and the conclusion is that their optical performance is as good as the basic matched filter. They have also been used in practical correlator systems [47, 48].

A further attraction of holographic lenses is that they can be prepared in an array format. This was investigated in [49] with a view to its application to an array of matched filters. The overall intensity efficiency is halved when a 4 × 4 array of lenses is used in place of a single lens.

3.7   Practical systems

General interest in practical correlators was stimulated by the advent of a real-time input device, the Hughes liquid crystal light valve (Section 4.4.2). Its applicability to robotic vision on the assembly line was demonstrated for high-contrast [50] and low-contrast [51] objects, using the matched filter correlator.

Subsequently, it was demonstrated that the AlGaAs injection laser could be used as the laser source in a matched filter correlator [52a]. A separate system with a helium neon laser was required for the fabrication of the matched filter on photographic plate. The implication of this demonstration for the development of compact correlators was underlined by suggestions for two types:

(1)   a cylindrical correlator of 200 cm³ and 2 W power consumption, and

(2)   a monolithic correlator of 45 cm³ and the same power consumption.†

---

†A monolithic correlator has now been constructed by the Perkin–Elmer Corporation [52b]. The optical and electro-optical hardware occupies 590 cm^3 and weighs less than 3 kg. The complete system requires only 3.5 W operating power.

The first portable correlator appeared in the literature in 1983 [47]. It was a matched filter correlator, employing four diode lasers, and measured 23 cm × 42 cm × 15 cm and weighed 8 kg. The associated electronics were of similar weight and the total power consumption was 55 W. The design incorporated folded optics to achieve the compact size. An assessment of the performance of this correlator was presented in [53]. The registration of the matched filter was a significant problem, which may limit this kind of system to dedicated tasks.

A more rugged system, which was built on a granite base measuring 60 cm × 25 cm, was described by a UK group in [54a].

The JTC system has been limited to optical bench studies [39, 40], although this has the potential of providing a multi-purpose practical correlator.

CHAPTER 4
SPATIAL LIGHT MODULATORS

4.1   Introduction

The widespread use of optical correlators depends upon the development of a real-time input device to replace photographic transparencies. This device is known as the **spatial light modulator (SLM)**. The majority of contemporary SLMs have developed from devices that were originally intended either for image storage or projection display, both with incoherent light read-out. The archetypal image storage device is the **PROM** (Pockels read-out optical modulator). The Pockels effect is an electro-optic effect, which is described in Section 4.2. Although a number of materials show this effect, 'the PROM' refers specifically to a BSO device. The **liquid crystal light valve (LCLV)** employs cadmium sulphide as the photoconductor, and was developed as a projection display. This is now known as 'the LCLV' and the new generation of dedicated SLMs based on this principle are referred to by their photo-sensitive constituent; for example, Si LCLV. The SLMs that are commercially available, and important for the system designer, are the Hughes LCLV, the Sumitomo PROM, the Litton LIGHT-MOD and the Hamamatsu MSLM.

Section 4.2 presents a description of the electro-optic effect employed in the majority of SLMs. Section 4.3 explains the parameters that charac-

47

terize the performance of devices. The principles of operation of a number of important devices are outlined in Sections 4.4 and 4.5; the former relates to those that are optically addressed and the latter to the electrically addressed ones.

4.2   Electro-optic effects

All the devices that employ an electro-optic crystal modulate the amplitude of the light by the following mechanism. A phase retardation plate is generated by the electric field applied to the crystal, and this rotates the polarization vector of the incident read-out light beam. An analyzer converts the polarization rotation into an amplitude change.

A phase retardation plate contains two orthogonal axes in the plane of the plate, which are labelled fast and slow. When the polarization vector of the read-out beam is aligned with either of these axes, it suffers no rotation. The nomenclature of the axes refers to the degree of phase retardation in the two cases; the wave whose polarization vector is aligned with the slow axis traverses a longer effective path length.

The retardation plate is characterized by the fraction of a given wavelength that corresponds to the difference in retardation between the two axes. For example, a half-wave retardation plate at 632.8 nm will give a phase difference of π radians between the fast and slow waves. Polarization vectors that are oriented between the two axes are rotated and, in the general case, are no longer linearly polarized. However, when the retardation is half-wave, then the linear polarization is maintained and the polarization vector is rotated about the slow axis (Figure 4.1). A special case occurs when the polarization vector bisects the two axes, when it is rotated by 90°. The analyzing prism can be oriented with its transmission axis either parallel (negative contrast) or perpendicular (positive contrast) to the initial polarization direction. The **Pockels effect** refers to a specific electro-optic interaction wherein the birefringence change is linear in the applied electric field.

4.3   SLM characterization

The performance figures of a number of SLMs are detailed in Tables 4.1 and 4.2. These have been selected to illustrate the variety of devices available, subject to the restriction that the performance has been measured rather than projected. A more comprehensive listing will be found in [55]. The **optically addressed SLMs (OASLMs)** and **electrically addressed SLMs (EASLMs)** are listed separately. Both types, in operation, impose a two-dimensional image on to a coherent light beam, rather like the lettering in a stick of rock. In the OASLMs, the image is written on the device using an incoherent light beam,

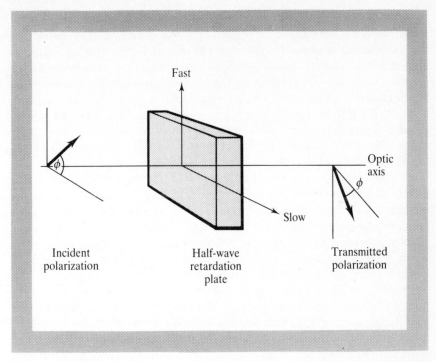

Fast

Optic
axis

ϕ

Slow

Incident
polarization

Half-wave
retardation
plate

Transmitted
polarization

Figure 4.1   The action of a phase retardation plate on the polarization vector of a mono-chromic light beam.

whereas, in the EASLMs, it is written either from a frame store or directly from a video camera.

The OASLMs require a minimum write beam intensity to develop an image, and this is known as the **threshold sensitivity**. The sensitivity that is tabulated is that at which a significant resolution and contrast are obtained; for example, when the read light level reaches 10% of its maximum intensity. The units for the sensitivity are power density in those cases where the electro-optic material does not store the image and energy density where the image is stored.

The frame time is the time required to replace one frame of information by another. Where the material response time is fast, the time required to write the information can be reduced, for example, by increasing the write light intensity on the OASLM structure. However, the frame time is invariably limited by the time required to remove the information, either by decay for non-storage devices or by erase for storage devices. Response times are conventionally quoted from 0–90% full response; the decay (or erase) times from 100–10% full response.

The resolution is measured experimentally. A sinusoidal grating is generated interferometrically and used as the writing beam. The fringe visibility of the grating on the read beam is measured. As the spatial frequency of the written grating is increased, the fringe visibility decreases to zero. The fringe visibility, normalized to 100% at low spatial frequency, is defined as the **modulation transfer function (MTF)** of the SLM. The resolution is quoted for 50% MTF, although this does not indicate the lower bound for practical usefulness. The resolution can also be measured in the Fourier plane rather than the image plane. The sinusoidal grating forms three spots: the 0, and ± 1 diffracted orders. The intensity of the first diffracted order is measured as a function of the spatial frequency. This method is experimentally easier than the imaging method at higher spatial frequencies and the quantitative relationship between the two is given in [56].

The contrast is expressed by the ratio of maximum light intensity to minimum intensity on the read side of the device. In two major respects, the contrast realized in system performance can be expected to fall short of the tabulated values. In the first place, the ratio is measured when the pattern is stabilized on the device, so that the lower contrast during writing and erasure is not taken into account. In the second place, the efficiency of the SLM depends on the amplitude or phase modulation of the recording (Section 5.2). The experimental configuration for maximum modulation is not always the same as that for maximum contrast. For example, when the electro-optic modulation generates a small angular rotation of the polarization vector, then the best contrast is found when the polarizer and analyzer are set to extinction; however, the largest modulation occurs when they are set at 45°.

The optical flatness of the device is important if phase errors are to be avoided. Typically, the manufacturer will provide either the peak-to-peak wavefront distortion or the r.m.s. distortion. The latter is an average over the active area of the device and is smaller in magnitude.

There is sometimes a discrepancy between the actual performance of OASLMs and the manufacturer's specifications. One problem is that the sensitivity, frame speed, resolution and contrast are not independent variables, and the optimization of one will prejudice the others. However, it is common practice on the manufacturer's part to specify the device according to the best value obtained in each case in separate experiments. A second problem is that, due to the non-uniformity of the device, a better set of specifications can be generated for a smaller area than the full aperture of the SLM. In Table 4.1, wherever possible, practical performance values have been used.

4.4   Optically addressed SLMs

4.4.1   Monolithic devices

BSO is a crystal that exhibits the Pockels effect. As the change in refractive index is proportional to the electric field, the change of phase of a light beam passing through the crystal is proportional to the voltage across the crystal.

Table 4.1 Optically addressed SLM characteristics.

SLM	Size	Mode of Operation	Sensitivity	Frame Time (ms)	Resolution (lp/mm)	Contrast Ratio	Optical Flatness	References
PROM	25 mm diam.	Reflection	5 μJ/cm^3	33	6	10^3:1	λ/10 (r.m.s.)	[58]
Priz	18 mm diam.	Transmission	5 μJ/cm^2	100	10			[60]
LCLV	(2 inch)^2	Reflection	8 mW/cm^2	80	25†	100:1	< 3λ/4 (pk-to-pk)	[54, 77]††
BSO LCLV	(15 mm)^2	Reflection	380 μW/cm^2	165	31	21:1	λ	[68]††
α-Si LCLV	(1.5 inch)^2	Reflection	20 μW/cm^2	50	35			[70]
Microchannel SLM ($\times$1699)	16 mm diam.	Reflection	30 nJ/cm^2	150	10	>10^3:1		[89]
α-Se ruticon	1.5 inch diam.	Reflection	1 μJ/cm^2	8	14	22:1		[85]
Phototitus (α-Se/DKDP)	~(2 cm)^2	Reflection	1 μJ/cm^2	1	20	10:1		[82]
Ferpic (CdS/PLZT)	7.5 mm diam.	Reflection	20 μJ/cm^2	0.1	20	4:1		[83]
Si LCLV p. diode	43 mm diam.	Reflection	40 μW/cm^2	25	12	20:1	4 λ	[64]

†Measured over circle of 16 mm diameter in centre of device.
††In these devices, the low frame time and high resolution can be obtained simultaneously at the write sensitivity quoted.

To change the phase by π radians, about 4 kV must be applied across the crystal [57]. This is called the **half-wave voltage**, because a half-wavelength retardation plate is formed. However, if the device is operated in the reflection mode, then the read light makes two passes through the crystal and only $\pi/2$ radians of retardation is required on each pass. Therefore, a reflection mode device has a lower half-wave voltage.

The structure of a reflection mode PROM is shown in Figure 4.2. The BSO has a (001) crystal orientation. A high voltage is applied and the crystal is flashed with UV light. The photogenerated electrons migrate to the anode until a reverse field, which is equal to the applied field, is created. The applied field is then reversed and the charge distribution is unaffected due to the high impedance. In this state, the uniform charge layer is selectively discharged when a light pattern is incident on the crystal. Alternatively, the image can be developed in a crystal in which there is no initial charge separation [58]. This latter mode of operation gives a poorer spatial frequency response.

The crystal is interrogated with a polarized 'read' beam and the degree of polarization rotation of each ray in the beam is related to the phase change the ray experienced when traversing the crystal. An analyzing prism converts the 'polarization' image into an amplitude distribution, which is a replica of the incoherent light image.

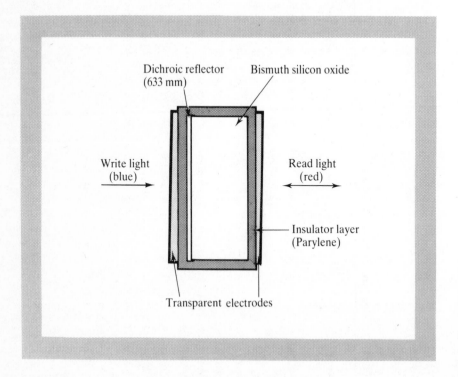

Figure 4.2   The PROM device.

A device of greater resolution has been fabricated, where the orientation of the BSO is along the (111) or (110) directions. This is known as the **Priz modulator** [59], and a thorough comparison with the PROM was made in [60a]. When this crystal cut is used, the internal electric fields oriented parallel to the plane of the crystal have an influence on the local optical constants and, hence, on the retardation properties. The spatial frequency response has a bandpass characteristic that drops to low values for uniform charge layers, because there is no planar electric field. This has the effect of enhancing the edges of the image and removing the areas of uniform contrast. The high frequency response declines more gradually than for the PROM. The remaining performance parameters are comparable. A more modern study, highlighting the extra functionality of the Priz device, is presented in [60b].

The theoretical limitations on the resolution of the PROM were examined in [61], which is now a classic paper in the field. A more modern treatment, which considers the effect of charge trapping in the bulk of the crystal and encompasses the Priz device, is covered in [62].

The second paper of the last reference draws attention to an important point in the comparison of PROM and Priz. Namely, that the only configuration that will give a pure amplitude modulation to the 'read' light is that of the PROM. The Priz configuration gives a combined amplitude/phase modulation. The Fourier spectrum of images formed on this type of device will be more extended than in the pure amplitude case, due to the presence of higher diffracted orders. As a consequence, the correlation peak may be more pronounced, but more susceptible to orientational/scale misalignments, because of the more extended Fourier plane spectrum.

4.4.2   Hybrid devices: liquid crystal/photodetector sandwich

The electro-optic effect in a nematic liquid crystal layer requires lower voltages (0–100 V AC at audio frequencies). When a layer of liquid crystal is combined with one or more layers that are photoactive and the structure is electroded on the outer layers, then an image can be written on to the liquid crystal layer.

The most important structure of this type is the Hughes LCLV [63] (Figure 4.3). The liquid crystal (BDH mixture E-7) is driven at 0–4 V r.m.s. and 10 kHz. The photodetector is formed by a layer of photoconductive CdS and an adjacent layer of CdTe (between the CdS and the liquid crystal). The layers form a heterojunction diode which is reverse biased in the dark state, so that no AC voltage is applied to the liquid crystal layer. When the CdS is illuminated, the charge on the diode leaks away during the relevant half-cycles of the AC waveform and an AC voltage appears across the liquid crystal layer. The magnitude of this AC voltage is related to the illumination intensity, and the change in the retardation property of the liquid crystal can be read by a polarized coherent beam in a similar manner to the PROM.

The low sensitivity and slow response of the CdS are the main

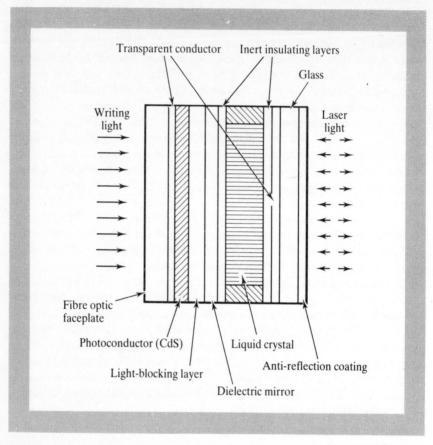

Figure 4.3   The Hughes liquid crystal light valve. (Reproduced by kind permission of Hughes Aircraft Company.)

disadvantages of the LCLV. Subsequent development work has led to the replacement of the CdS/CdTe system by Si/SiO_2 [64]. A phosphorous-implanted microdiode array prevents the lateral diffusion of charge at the interface and, therefore, maintains a good resolution. An asymmetric AC electrical waveform drives the sandwich. During the period when the junction is reverse biased, the silicon is depleted and photogenerated electrons accumulate at the microdiode array. Subsequently, a short forward bias period removes the accumulated charge by recombination. The temporal asymmetry of the waveform maximizes the 'active' state of the light valve; that is, the charge accumulation phase. This is allowed because of the relatively fast recombination rate of the photogenerated charges.

An alternative Si LCLV is described in [65]. The single crystal silicon is driven into depletion by the AC waveform applied to the cell. During the depletion periods, the impedance of the silicon is matched to the liquid crystal. High sensitivity, contrast and resolution are reported.

If a GaAs crystal is employed [66], the intrinsic resistivity is sufficiently high so that active depletion is not required, and the cell can be operated at lower AC voltages. In common with the silicon device, the resolution is limited by the high mobility of the carriers and the consequent large lateral spreading [67].

A contrasting situation is revealed when BSO is used as the photoconductor. Here, the quantum efficiency is low, but the mobility is also low, due to the large density of trapping centres. Consequently, higher resolutions can be achieved (see Table 4.1). The low sensitivity in this device does not allow the facility of CRT address, in contrast to the LCLV. In addition, charge detrapping limits the speed, as in the case of CdS.

A good compromise for high resolution and sensitivity is to use amorphous silicon [70]. The layer thickness and doping levels can be varied to optimize the several operating parameters. Unfortunately, it is not known, at present, to what extent the traps will limit the framing speed.

Other photoconductors that have been used in these devices include CdSe TV-camera targets [71], ZnS [72, 73], Se [74], As_2S_3 [75] and $AsSe_4$ [76]. A useful summary is presented in [78].

Although each worker uses a different liquid crystal material, there are a limited number of liquid crystal effects that can be employed. For example, the LCLV employs the hybrid field effect, while the BSO LCLV in [69, 80] employs controlled birefringence (known also as the S effect). The hybrid field effect requires that the liquid crystal director is aligned parallel to the cell surface (planar or homogeneous alignment) and that the angle between the alignment directions on the two surfaces is 45°. When the voltage across the cell is zero, a light beam, which is polarized either parallel or perpendicular to the alignment direction on the front surface, is reflected from the cell with the same direction of polarization. A dark off-state results when the reflected beam traverses an analyzer set to extinction. However, when a voltage is applied to the cell, the uniform twist is disrupted and the liquid crystal director tilts. The cell becomes birefringent and will rotate the polarization of the read light. This produces a bright on-state. The advantage of this configuration is high-contrast performance that is independent of thickness [79]. On the other hand, the controlled birefringence effect requires planar alignment with no twist. In this configuration, the polarization direction of the light should be oriented at 45° with respect to the alignment direction to achieve polarization rotation. It is more difficult to establish good extinction, which will require a rotation of exactly 90°. Hence, contrast ratio suffers, and good thickness uniformity is important. However, the voltage threshold is lower than the hybrid effect and the birefringence is stronger, enabling the use of thinner layers and, hence, faster operation. In both cases, a mixed phase/amplitude modulation is realized. In the case of controlled birefringence, pure phase modulation can be realized when the polarization direction is parallel to the alignment direction [73]. In general, the Russian work tends to favour the S effect, while Western work favours the hybrid field effect. Other liquid crystal effects that involve transitions between scattering and non-scattering states are not so useful for coherent light systems because they add noise to the phase of the light wave. For example, the dynamic scattering mode and cholesteric-to-nematic transition [74, 76] are restricted to display applications.

The main disadvantage of the nematic liquid crystals is their slow response times. The switch-on times can be decreased by increasing the drive voltage. However, the switch-off time is relaxation dependent and limits the cycle time to tens of milliseconds. An alternative drive scheme, where two frequencies are applied sequentially to drive both switch-on and switch-off, has taken the cycle time down to 200 μs [78]. A further increase in speed requires moving away from nematic materials to smectic C ferroelectric liquid crystals, where a further order of magnitude increase can be realized [81]. The director is rotated by about 45° when a DC voltage is applied to the cell and returns to its former orientation when the polarity of the DC voltage is reversed. Consequently, the electro-optic response is two-state, or binary, as opposed to the analogue response of the nematics, which provides a grey scale.

There is a light blocking layer and a dielectric mirror between the liquid crystal and the photoconductor in reflection mode devices. These degrade the voltage transfer to the liquid crystal and are, generally, difficult to design. However, they can be neglected in special cases where the photoconductor strongly absorbs the read light [74]. Where the photoconductor is transparent to the read light, it is better to employ a transmission device, where spurious reflections do not degrade the contrast ratio.

4.4.3   Other hybrid devices

When the photoconductor is interfaced to an electro-optic crystal of the Pockels effect type, then a device of much lower sensitivity than the liquid crystal hybrid results. This is due to the large half-wave voltage (about 1 kV) compared with switching voltages for liquid crystals (about 1 V). Even with the development of crystals of lower half-wave voltage, there is commonly a corresponding increase in the dielectric constant, so that the charge required and, hence, the optical energy, shows little variation. However, the good optical uniformity of the single crystal is an advantage here, and this device structure has been exploited in the Phototitus [82], the Ferpic [83] and more recently in a design study for a silicon photodiode/KD*P SLM [84].

An alternative configuration for these electro-optic crystals is in association with a photoemitter and microchannel plate. When a DC voltage is applied to this structure, the photoelectrons are amplified by the micro-channel plate and charge up the crystal. In the Hamamatsu device, the MSLM, the electrons impinge finally on a $LiNbO_3$ crystal. The large half-wave voltage of $LiNbO_3$ (1.2 kV) means that a large charge has to be accumulated on the surface of the crystal to achieve the full dynamic range. Now, the current in the microchannel plate is limited to about 2 μA [88]. If the thickness of the crystal is increased, its capacitance is reduced, and less charge is required to attain the necessary voltage. However, the spatial resolution, which is approximately the inverse of the crystal thickness, is consequently reduced. Therefore, either the frame speed or the resolution are restricted in this device.

If the electro-optic crystal is replaced by a thin metallized membrane, then the resolution of the plate can be maintained, together with high frame speeds. This is the principle of the photoemitter membrane SLM [87], where the membrane is a 50 nm nitrocellulose layer with 80 nm of metallization. The frame rate is predicted to be 1 kHz and a quantum-limited sensitivity of 0.5 nJ/cm^2 is envisaged.

Two further types of opto-mechanical devices involve the interfacing of either a thermoplastic or an elastomer layer to a photoconductor. The thermoplastic device requires a heating cycle to develop the image and, due to its high resolution, it is more appropriately classified with the recording devices in the next chapter. One elastomer structure, the α-Se ruticon, is a particular type of ruticon where a metallization layer on the surface of the elastomer is responsible for the reflection of the read-out light. A good elastomer would produce a deformation of 0.1 μm when the overall voltage across the device is 300 V [85]. This is comparable to the Pockels effect hybrid where a path length difference of 0.3 μm is obtained for overall voltages of 1 kV. The ruticon device, in common with all opto-mechanical devices, modulates the phase of the read-out light, which generates harmonic distortion at large amplitudes. It has found practical application in prototype projection TV systems [86], where the image quality is of primary importance. Consequently, the maximum amplitude of deformation considered was about one-sixth of visible light wavelength. In the application to spatial light modulation, the diffraction efficiency is of primary importance, so that larger deformations are required. In common with a number of types of SLM, it is the time required for erase that limits frame speed. This is about 1 ms [84].

4.5   Electrically addressed SLMs

4.5.1   Pixellated devices

The multiplexed liquid crystal display is a convenient stand-in for an electrically addressed input device [6]. A thin film transistor at each pixel generates the few volts required to switch the liquid crystal. The data is clocked into a row of transistors in parallel by using a strobe voltage on the row address line. The transistor maintains the pixel voltage while the other rows are being addressed, so that a frame of information can be clocked in, in less than the response time of the liquid crystal. This is the active matrix address principle. Alternatively, where a faster liquid crystal effect is employed, such as the binary switch of the ferroelectric liquid crystals, then each row can be switched in the response time of the liquid crystal, and modest framing rates

Table 4.2   Electrically addressed SLM characteristics.

SLM	Size	Resolution† (lp/mm)	Frame Time	Contrast Ratio	Optical Flatness	References
LIGHT-MOD						
256–03	(20 mm)^2	256 × 256	1 s (10 ms)††	10^3:1	λ/2	
128–03	(10 mm)^2	128 × 128	250 ms (2 ms)††		λ/2	[90]
48–05	(8.5 mm)^2	48 × 48	33 ms (700 µs)††		λ/2	
DMD	(6.4 mm)^2	(9.8)	16 ms	30:1		[97]
CLV	(20 mm)^2	800 × 500	33 ms	10^2:1		[101]
e-beam DKDP (Titus)	(50–75 mm)^2	(20)	33 ms	10^2–10^3:1	<λ/4	[100]
e-beam thermoplastic (Lumatron)	(1.5 inch)^2	(70)	1 s			[103]

†Or number of pixels.
††Frame rates for line-parallel address.

maintained [81]. In this case, the cell construction is much simpler. Row and column electrodes are photolithographically defined on the two glass plates that form the cell walls, the rows on one and the columns on the other. The simpler pixel structure eases fabrication and produces negligible pixel diffraction. The latter effect is characterized by an array of spots in the Fourier plane, which are independent of the image displayed. As these must be filtered out, to avoid spurious correlation signals, this causes a consequent loss in light throughput efficiency. The phase imperfections of a display-quality device result in 'space variance' effects which limit the translational invariance of the correlator approach. Although there are methods for correcting this, it is preferable to fabricate devices suitable for coherent light applications. The Hughes CCD LCLV is such an example.

The CCD-addressed LCLV [64] is constructed as an electroded sandwich of silicon and nematic liquid crystal. The CCD array is fabricated on the outermost layer of the silicon. The frame of information is collected and stored as charge packets in the array. When all the array gates are biased into accumulation, the charge packets are injected into the substrate and are collected in the depleted region close to the liquid crystal layer. These generate the electro-optic effect in the liquid crystal. It is projected that a $(1000)^2$ pixel device will operate at frame rates of 100 Hz. A 256×256 device has been operated successfully in the laboratory at Hughes Research.

The LIGHT-MOD [91] is a thin magnetic garnet film that has been grown on a non-magnetic substrate and then etched into an array using semiconductor photolithographic techniques. The magnetization in each pixel can be switched independently between two anti-parallel states perpendicular to the plane of the film. The polarization of a light beam propagating through the pixel is rotated either clockwise or anti-clockwise depending on the direction of magnetization (Faraday effect). The light absorption in the garnet film is about 50%, and, due to the small polarization rotation, less than 10% of the light is converted to the orthogonal polarization. In addition, the lack of a grey scale is a disadvantage for analogue pattern recognition, but schemes for overcoming this have been outlined [92]. A similar device (LISA), made from a different garnet material, requires a heat pulse at each pixel to assist the magnetic switching [93].

Early studies on the ferroelectric PLZT have been summarized in [94]. The advantage of the ferroelectric state (as with the ferromagnetic state in the garnets) is the memory effect. The lack of sharpness in the switching characteristics of the macroscopic polarization allows crosstalk when multiplex methods are used for matrix address of a single crystal two-dimensional array. Therefore, such arrays are preferentially addressed by silicon transistors at each pixel [95]. When fast phototransistors are used, there is the potential for either optical or electrical address at frame times of 10 μs. Moreover, it is not difficult to envisage some pre-processing operation on the image using additional logic/memory circuitry in the silicon. An alternative ferroelectric is gadolinium molybdate which is anisotropic in the plane perpendicular to the ferroelectric polarization vector; that is, the plane of the device [96]. Therefore, it forms a retardation plate, as in Pockels effect devices.

The deformable mirror device (DMD) [97] is a thin reflecting membrane that covers an array of **MOS transistors**. The membrane is separated from the array by polysilicon pillars, which surround each pixel producing an air gap < 1 μm. The floating source of each MOS transistor is directly beneath the unsupported area of the membrane and deforms the membrane by electrostatic attraction when it is charged. The mechanism of light modulation in this device differs from all the previous devices, which operate as variable retardation plates. In this case, the phase of the light wave is modulated. The consequences of this, in the Fourier plane, are an increased first-order diffraction efficiency, but with the appearance of higher harmonics. This device has also been modified for optical address [98]. A survey of micromechanical devices is included in [99].

4.5.2   Electron-beam addressed devices

Electron-beam (e-beam) address is a direct method for building up the charge distribution on an electro-optic crystal. Beam currents of the order of microamperes are equivalent to a laser beam of 1 mW incident on a photoconductor sandwich, where the quantum efficiency of the photoconductor is about 1%. However, the complication of a sandwich structure is avoided. The theoretical limitations of the e-beam addressed device are detailed in [61]. The sensitivity of the device is defined as the voltage that can be established across the crystal by a unit modulation charge density on one face of the crystal. When the spatial frequency of the modulation is low, the sensitivity is proportional to the thickness of the crystal; when it is high, it is independent of the thickness and is inversely proportional to the spatial frequency. Therefore, decreasing the thickness of the crystal only increases the spatial resolution at the expense of reducing the low frequency sensitivity.

Historically, the first device to make an impact in this field employed potassium dideuterium phosphate (DKDP) as the electro-optic crystal. This crystal can be cooled near to the ferroelectric state at $-50°$C by a two-stage Peltier cooler [100]. The advantage of this is that the dielectric constant becomes anisotropic, so that the resolution of the device is increased in accordance with the theory in [61].

Among the devices that do not employ an electro-optic crystal, the most important, historically, is the coherent light valve (CLV) [101]. The e-beam deforms the surface of an oil film due to electrostatic forces. The oil film is supported on a transparent disk and is constantly refreshed by rotating the disk in an oil sump. The depressions generated in the surface of the film cause a phase modulation of the transmitted light. (An interesting oil film device where the film is interfaced to an optical absorber, and deforms as a consequence of the dependence of surface tension on temperature, has been recorded in [102]. However, low sensitivity and resolution limit practical application.)

4.6 Present research

There has been a greater degree of success with optically addressed SLMs than with their electrically addressed counterparts. This is probably due to the longer history of OASLMs. The rationale for improving the sensitivity of OASLMs is that the correlator might be employed in a 'staring' mode for tracking fast-moving objects. (With the LCLV, tracking is successful for a well-illuminated object, travelling on a conveyor belt at 25 cm/s [51].) However, the wider applications of optical processing systems depend on the development of an interface to the electronic world. The display industry has an important influence on opportunities for EASLMs. For example, it has provided a source of cheap, active matrix liquid crystal displays, which are being upgraded for coherent optical application, and it has generated the LIGHT-MOD, which is the first commercial EASLM. It is hoped that more will follow.

CHAPTER 5
HOLOGRAPHIC RECORDING DEVICES

5.1 Introduction

The optical recording devices of high resolution have been separated from the OASLMs because they are used within the correlator system and not, in general, as input devices. The system requirements for the resolution of the device that is to record the Fourier plane spectrum in a correlator may be summarized as follows. To record both the phase and amplitude of the spectrum, a hologram is formed by interference with a plane reference wave. The phase structure of the spectrum does not have a high spatial frequency and, therefore, at first sight, a hologram of low resolution will suffice. However, it is preferable to employ a high-resolution holographic medium, as a hologram of high spatial frequency ensures that the reconstruction beams are well separated. In particular, the correlation beam of low intensity is distinct from the object beam of relatively high intensity. The spatial frequency of the recording can be adjusted experimentally, according to the intersection angle of the recording beams. A convenient device resolution is 200 lp/mm (Section 3.3.2).

In addition to having a high resolution, it should, ideally, be possible to write holograms on the device, *in situ*, at the framing speed of the correlator. This would allow the most flexible system: a JTC where both the scene and the template may vary. However, appropriate devices do not yet exist, due to the short development time of this field. The standard recording material, at present, is silver halide emulsion, on which the fixed template matched filter can be recorded. The properties of this material have been studied in the context of holography and stand as a paradigm for the study of other promising materials. The discussion of photographic materials is treated in Section 5.4. To increase the diffraction efficiency of the recording, a phase hologram can be formed in gelatin, either by bleaching an amplitude hologram or by using dichromated gelatin. Such devices, which are beginning to appear in correlators, are discussed in Section 5.5. Section 5.6 discusses three dissimilar categories of materials, which are grouped together because each is a small area of interest: they are the photopolymers, photochromics and photodichroics. The thermoplastics, where the primary photoresponse is a structural deformation, are treated in Section 5.7. The final section treats the increasingly important photorefractive crystals, such as BSO, which is employed in the demonstrator correlator of the appendix. The characteristics of the materials discussed are shown in Table 5.1.

In all these materials, the optically induced refractive index change is smaller than desired. In the case of the photorefractives, accommodation is made by increasing the thickness, so that a more pronounced optical effect is forthcoming. The diffraction theory of 'thick' materials differs from that of two-dimensional screens ('thin' holograms). Therefore, the theories are reviewed in the next section, followed by a discussion in Section 5.3, of a particular problem that results when thick recording materials are used.

5.2   Diffraction efficiency of thin and thick holograms

The ratio of the light intensity of the reconstructed beam to that of the interrogation beam is the **diffraction efficiency (DE)** of the hologram. The material properties that influence this efficiency can be derived from the simplest case of diffraction by a periodic structure; namely, a plane wave incident upon a sinusoidal modulation. The modulation may operate on either the amplitude or the phase of the light wave, or a mixture of both. The efficiency in each case can be calculated from a Fourier transform of the relevant aperture function, in those cases where the hologram is 'thin' (see later).

In the case of amplitude modulation, the aperture function is:

$$f(x) = \frac{T_o}{2}(1 + m\cos 2\pi\nu_o x) = \frac{T_o}{2}\left[1 + \frac{m}{2}\left(e^{2\pi\nu_o x} + e^{-2\pi\nu_o x}\right)\right]$$

Table 5.1 Holographic recording materials.

Recording Material	Sensitivity ($\mu J/cm^2$)	Wavelength Range (Recording)	Thickness (μ)	Resolution (10^3 lp/mm)	Speed (ms)	Diffraction Efficiency (%)	Amplitude (A) or Phase (P) Modulation
Silver halide emulsion	10	blue to 750 nm	6–17	≤5	100	6	A
Dichromated gelatin	10^5	UV to 520 nm	1–13	>5		80	P
Thermoplastics	100	blue to 1.15 μm	0.2–10	0.05–2.5 (peak)	250	32	P
Photorefractive BSO	300	blue	0.4–2 mm	0.03–1	20 (at 10 mW/cm^2)	0.3 (zero field) 25 (9 kV/cm)	P
Photochromics	10^5	488, 514, 633	variable	>3	very fast	1	A
Photopolymer [116] DMP-128	10^4	visible	1–30	≤1.6	~ min	90	P
Photoresistors	10^5	UV to 500 nm	≤4	>1	100	10	P

where T_o is the average transmittance, m is the modulation depth $(0 < m < 1)$, and ν_o is the spatial frequency of the modulation.

The Fourier transform consists of three δ-functions: one at zero frequency and two at $u = \pm \nu_o$. The latter convey the important information concerning the modulation, and one of these is designated the reconstructed beam. The amplitude of the reconstructed beam is $T_o m/4$. Therefore, the diffraction efficiency is $T_o^2 m^2/16$. With full modulation depth ($m = 1$), and 100% transmission, the (maximum) efficiency is 6%. If the light beam is, in addition, attenuated in the medium, then the efficiency is reduced by the attenuation.

Alternatively, phase modulation is commonly produced by a refractive index modulation. For example:

$$n(x) = n_o + \Delta n \cos 2\pi\nu_o x$$

generates a phase modulation given by:

$$\phi(x) = \frac{2\pi n(x)t}{n_o\lambda} = \frac{2\pi t}{\lambda}\left[1 + \left(\frac{\Delta n}{n_o}\right)\cos 2\pi\nu_o x\right] = \phi_o + \Delta\phi \cos 2\pi\nu_o x$$

where t is the thickness of the hologram.

The aperture function is given by:

$$g(x) = \exp[i\phi(x)]$$

and the Fourier transform is a series of δ-functions at $u = 0, \pm \nu_o, \pm 2\nu_o$, etc. The amplitude of the nth harmonic is $J_n(\Delta\phi)$. Consequently, the diffraction efficiency is $[J_1(\Delta\phi)]^2$. For small refractive index modulations, the efficiency is:

$$\eta = \frac{(\Delta\phi)^2}{4} = \left(\frac{\pi\Delta nt}{n_o\lambda}\right)^2$$

The maximum efficiency that can be achieved is the maximum value of $[J_1(\Delta\phi)]^2$; that is, 33.8%. This pertains when $2\pi \Delta nt = 1.8 \, n_o\lambda$. Again, uniform attenuation reduces the efficiency accordingly.

In contrast, in the theory of thick holograms, the cumulative action of the grating modulation on the reconstructed beam as it passes through the material is considered. The coupled wave theory [104] has been frequently applied. A consequence of this theory is that diffraction efficiency is considerably enhanced when the interrogation beam strikes the recorded grating at a particular angle, called the **Bragg angle**. At the Bragg angle, the wave vectors of the interrogation and reconstructed beams, and the wave vector of the grating, form an isosceles triangle (Figure 5.1). The reconstructed rays from each section of the grating add coherently. The maximum diffraction

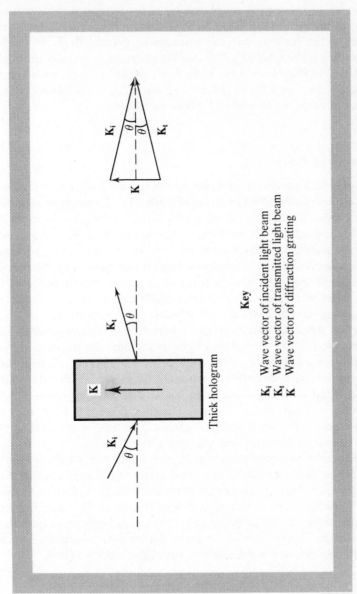

Figure 5.1 Bragg diffraction from thick holograms (where K_i is the wave vector of the incident light beam, K_t is the wave vector of the transmitted light beam and K is the wave vector of the diffraction grating).

efficiency for phase holograms rises to 100% in these circumstances. However, the maximum for amplitude holograms drops to 4%, due to increased attenuation.

The distinction between optically thin and thick gratings is not a sharp one. However, a convenient simplification is to consider a reconstructed beam passing through the thickness of the hologram. If it traverses more than two fringes of the grating, then the structure is optically thick. In mathematical terms, it is the ratio of $\lambda d/\Lambda^2$ that is important, where d is the thickness and Λ is the wavelength of the grating. When this is greater than 1, then the grating is thick. For a 5 μm grating and visible light, a thickness greater than 50 μm corresponds to a 'thick' recording medium.

5.3   Spatial variance

A hologram is formed when two beams of light with a given phase relationship interfere in a medium that records light intensity. The phase relationship of the two beams should be constant in time but will vary spatially in accordance with the angle of intersection of the beams, and the information carried on the beams. The recording is complete, in the sense that either beam can be reconstructed from the recording when it is irradiated by the partner beam that is now the interrogation beam. This is the principle of the FPC. When the angle of incidence of the interrogation beam deviates from the angle pertaining to the recording, the efficiency of reconstruction is diminished. Hence, when the quarry occupies a position in the scene that differs from its position in the recording of the hologram, the intensity of the correlation beam is diminished. The tracking of the quarry is accomplished by measuring the lateral deviation of the correlation spot, which is due to the angular deviation of the reconstructed beam. The tracking range will be limited by the reduced reconstruction efficiency (Figure 5.2). This is an example of the 'spatial variance' of a practical system, in contrast to the spatial invariance of the mathematical formalism.

The decrease in reconstruction efficiency can be directly related to the thickness of the hologram [105]. For small deviations, it is proportional to the squared power of the product of the normalized thickness and the angular deviation. (The thickness is normalized with respect to the wavelength of light in the medium.) Experimentally, the situation can be more complex than this, and changes in the shape of the correlation peak, in addition to an exaggerated decrease in the peak height, have been reported [106].

5.4   Silver halide emulsion

This material has been well researched for holographic recording. It has a high sensitivity due to gain in the development process. The gelatin emulsion

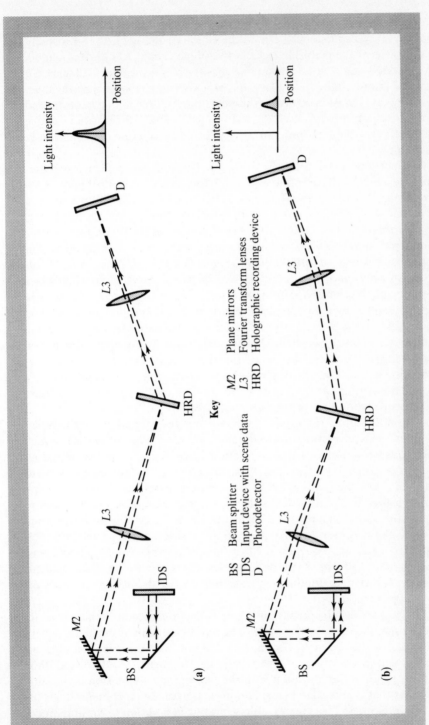

Key

BS	Beam splitter	M2	Plane mirrors
IDS	Input device with scene data	L3	Fourier transform lenses
D	Photodetector	HRD	Holographic recording device

Figure 5.2 The effect of spatial variance: the correlation spot intensity in (b) is reduced with respect to the intensity in (a).

is interspersed with crystals of silver bromide. When a small number of silver ions in a crystal are reduced due to the action of the light, the subsequent development of the emulsion reduces the whole crystal. Gains of about 10^6 are generated, and the corresponding sensitivity is typically 10 μJ/cm^2. To effect the photoreduction of silver ions at wavelengths longer than the blue, sensitizing dyes must be added to the emulsion. This technique has extended the photoresponse to beyond 700 nm [107]. Thick emulsions are not available commercially, although they can be engineered by soaking the emulsion in water [108].

The transfer characteristic of the emulsion can be conveniently represented by a plot of the amplitude transmission versus the logarithm of exposure (Figure 5.3(a)). The diffraction efficiency of the emulsion will be a maximum when the magnitude of the slope of this curve is a maximum, and this occurs at $T = 0.4$ for a variety of emulsions [107]. Two alternative representations of the transfer characteristic are the optical density versus log exposure, or **Hurter–Driffield curve** (Figure 5.3(b)), and the transmission versus exposure curve (Figure 5.3(c)). The T versus E curve is important when it is necessary to consider non-linear effects as a noise source. The curve is then represented by a polynomial expansion of the exposure about the bias exposure [4, 109]. The Fourier transform of this expansion is a series of multiple correlations, which are located in the correlation plane. Certain of these increase the lateral extent of the simple autocorrelation and cross-correlation peaks. The practical method for correcting these anomalies is to increase the grating carrier frequency to separate the cross-correlation from the autocorrelation by a greater distance [109].

In addition to the effects of non-linear transfer, there is the noise generated by the discrete nature of the silver grains. This generates scattering, which adds random noise to the correlation signal. Since the scatter decreases with the distance from the optic axis, the SNRs at the correlation spot is improved when the grating carrier frequency is increased. This scatter has been measured in a particular case [110], and based on these results, an estimate of the scatter in a practical correlator can be made. The distance from the optic axis is chosen to correspond to the position of the correlation spot relating to a grating frequency of 200 lp/mm, wavelength of 0.5 μm and lens focal length of 250 mm. Then the noise intensity is about 10^{-6} of the incident intensity. If this is the dominant noise source, then a diffraction efficiency of 10^{-5} will produce a SNR of 10.

The main disadvantage of using silver halide emulsions is that the plate must be removed for development. The developed plate must be realigned to the tolerances given in Section 3.3.2. However, the new methods of *in situ* heat processing, or monobath development, would avoid this problem [108]. A complication with the photographic emulsion is the surface relief that is generated by the tanning action of the reaction products of certain developers. This creates a phase grating in addition to the amplitude grating.

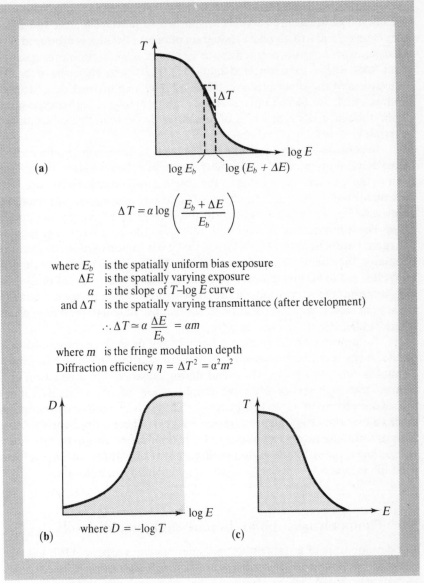

$$\Delta T = \alpha \log \left(\frac{E_b + \Delta E}{E_b} \right)$$

where E_b is the spatially uniform bias exposure
        ΔE is the spatially varying exposure
        α is the slope of T–$\log E$ curve
and ΔT is the spatially varying transmittance (after development)

$$\therefore \Delta T \simeq \alpha \, \frac{\Delta E}{E_b} = \alpha m$$

where m is the fringe modulation depth
Diffraction efficiency $\eta = \Delta T^2 = \alpha^2 m^2$

Figure 5.3   Characteristic curves for photographic emulsion.

5.5   Gelatin phase structures

A phase hologram can be formed by modulating either the thickness or the dispersive part of the refractive index. The thickness relief that is generated in the gelatin of silver halide emulsions is a decreasing function of spatial frequency, and drops to zero at 600 lp/mm [107]. It is not employed directly, for this reason, but will accompany the refractive index modulation produced by bleaching. The bleaching reagents are chosen to produce a large refractive index change, and a thick phase hologram of high efficiency is produced. For example, exposure to bromine vapour generates a diffraction efficiency of about 70%, with < 10% scattered light [111]. This scattering is due to the discrete nature of the silver bromide particles. The high diffraction efficiency requires a high pre-bleach optical density, and, therefore, higher exposures. Hence, the sensitivity is an order of magnitude lower than that of amplitude holograms.

In contrast, layers of gelatin that are sensitized by ammonium dichromate (DCG) show minimal light scatter, but require larger optical intensities. Both of these properties are due to the absence of a granular structure. The dichromate is dissolved in the colloid (about 5% by weight) and this renders it photosensitive. The exact nature of the photochemical reaction is not understood, but it results in a difference of refractive index between exposed and unexposed areas of about 10^{-3}. This is sufficient to be useful in the memory correlator for character recognition [112]. The hologram remains *in situ*. However, red light must be used to read the hologram, to avoid erasing it. This increases the aberrations in the reconstructed beam by some power of the scaling factor, which is the ratio of the reconstruction to recording wavelength [113].

To improve the diffraction efficiency and desensitize the emulsion, a development procedure consisting of a wash and fast dry using isopropyl alcohol is employed [114]. The rapid drying enhances the diffraction efficiency, and suggests an effective amplification of the refractive index modulation by up to $40 \times$. It is believed that this is due to the formation of cracks along the Bragg planes (grating fringes). These holograms exhibit a high dynamic range and resolution. Their application in the memory correlator has recently appeared in the literature [115]. Unfortunately, a short shelf life (about a few hours) has stifled commercial exploitation.

5.6   Photopolymers, photochromics and photodichroics

The development of a stable photopolymer system, recently [116], has simplified the generation of phase holograms of high diffraction efficiency. The recording is based on the dye-sensitized photopolymerization of a vinyl monomer. The monomer is dispersed in a polymer matrix which can be coated on glass in layers of variable thickness, from 1 to 30 μm. The mechanics of photopolymerization have been analyzed in other systems [117]. There are two important processes: the diffusion of initiator molecules to regions of high light intensity, and the orientation of the polymer chains.

The photochromics are reusable, and the modern types (for example, the fulgides) can be recycled thousands of times [118]. Upon irradiation by light of a short wavelength, which is commonly UV, the material is sensitized to light of a longer wavelength, and vice versa. By appropriate materials selection, the absorption peak of the sensitized form can be chosen close to a laser wavelength. The light mediates a spatial reconfiguration of the electrons either at the molecular level (in the organic photochromics) or between traps (in the inorganic photochromics). The effect in organics generally involves the formation and cleavage of benzene rings in aromatic compounds. The inorganics are large gap insulators and semiconductors, which have been doped to give absorption bands in the visible. As a consequence of the electronic process, a high resolution and speed characterize the effect. However, the refractive index modulation is small because there is no gain in the material, as there is in the photopolymer. A typical quantum efficiency for the fulgides would be one molecular reconfiguration for every four photons [119].

The photodichroic effect describes the alignment of certain colour centres in doped alkali halides and the consequent anisotropic absorption of the read-out illumination; that is, the absorption depends on the direction of polarization. One virtue of such material, in this context, is that the same wavelength can be used to write and read the hologram. Hence, aberrations are reduced. The practical application of this material to the JTC has been cited in [120, 121]. The disadvantages include the need for cooling to extend the recycle lifetime, hydroscopy requiring care in handling, and poor optical finish due to the softness of the halides.

5.7 Thermoplastics

A **thermoplastic (TP)** is a material that can be softened by heating above its flow temperature, usually in excess of 100°C. When a charge pattern is imposed on one surface of a TP layer, and the other surface is at ground potential, then the softening will result in the deformation of the surface in accordance with the pattern. Subsequent cooling returns the plastic to its rigid state, and the pattern is retained. Erasure is accomplished by further heating.

Two forms of addressing are employed in practical devices. The charge pattern can be written directly by an electron beam, or a photoconductor–thermoplastic bilayer can be charged uniformly by a corona and optically addressed. Current pulses of between 10 and 100 ms duration heat the layer to imprint the recording, and longer heat pulses are used to erase.

The valuable properties of these devices in this application are a high diffraction efficiency and a bandpass spatial frequency response. A deformed surface behaves as a thin phase hologram, which has a theoretical diffraction efficiency of 34%. Experimental diffraction efficiencies of 24% and 33% have been recorded in the photoconductor [122] and e-beam [123] devices, respectively. The MTF of the device drops at low spatial frequencies because the flow of material over a large distance is limited by viscosity, for a given development time. At high frequencies, the surface tension is the limiting factor. The peak of the modulation transfer function is roughly at the reciprocal of twice the thickness of the thermoplastic layer.

Photo-thermoplastic film is available in 35 mm size, and cameras have been built [124], or are available commercially [125], for exposing and developing the film *in situ*. Alternatively, a commercial camera using a recyclable material is available [126]. Matched filtering has been demonstrated [127], and, in addition, holographic recording in the JTC configuration [128]. The material can also be used as an incoherent-to-coherent converter, but this requires that the input image is multiplied by a regular grating, which acts as a spatial carrier [129]. More recently, a Brown and Lohmann type computer-generated hologram has been successfully recorded on an e-beam device [123].

The main drawbacks of this material have been a limited amount of recycling and the tendency for random deformation, known as 'frost' noise. However, they are now no longer a serious problem. Its application is limited to those correlators where rapid update of the hologram is not required.

5.8   Photorefractives

The photorefractive effect is associated with crystals that exhibit a significant linear electro-optic effect. Electrons are released by the photo-ionization of impurities in the crystal. When the crystal is irradiated with a spatially inhomogeneous light beam, the electrons migrate from the areas of high irradiance to those of low irradiance. This migration is a consequence of diffusion. The diffusion proceeds until the internal field generated is of sufficient strength to counteract it. It is this internal field that is responsible for the refractive index modulation, via the linear electro-optic effect. The diffusion length of the electrons is typically less than the fringe spacing (for example, $0.6 \mu m$ in BSO [130]). Therefore, an electric field is applied parallel to the wave vector of the grating to increase the distance that the electrons travel before trapping. The diffraction efficiency improves in proportion to the square of the electric field, but never to the high efficiency expected of thick phase holograms. The refractive index modulation is out of phase with the spatial information on the incident light wavefront (Figure 5.4).

A wide variety of materials exhibit this effect [131], but the availability of large samples with good optical quality is poor. A synthesis program has recently been announced for the more promising materials [132]. Most work over the last decade has been done using BSO. The sensitivity of different materials is proportional to the cube power of their refractive index [131]. However, the response time of the crystal is proportional to the dielectric constant. Therefore, crystals that are more sensitive, are slower. The dielectric relaxation time is the ratio of the dielectric permittivity to the conductivity. Since the crystals are insulators, by and large, their dark conductivity is

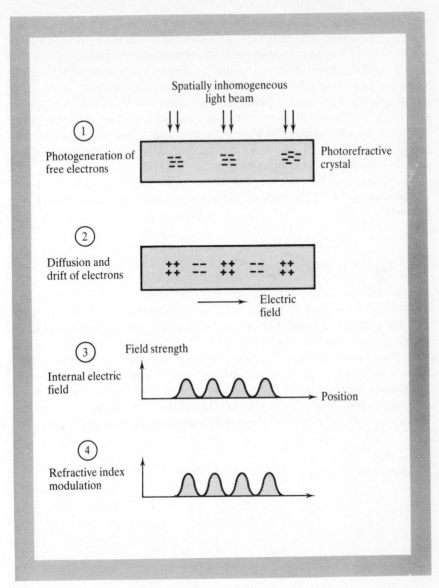

Figure 5.4 The photorefractive effect.

high, and the recording is durable unless actively erased. The conductivity under irradiation is proportional to the light intensity, so that the product of response time and light intensity is a constant.

Four noise problems associated with this effect will be mentioned here. In common with all recording materials where the recording is developing during the writing period, there is a scattering associated with self-diffraction. This leads to a distorted recording and limits the number of holograms that can be stored. A related, and more serious, potential problem in practice is that any mechanically produced random vibration of the light beams gives a partial erasure of the recording and the production of new recordings that are spatially displaced from the original. These interfere with the diffraction of the light and produce a time-varying correlation spot intensity. If the decay of the grating were faster, then this effect would be ameliorated. Alternatively, a pulsed laser beam can be used to write the hologram. The third noise source is the generation of higher harmonics due to the asymmetry of the fringe pattern when an electric field is applied. A fourth potential source of noise is scattering off material defects.

The main problem with photorefractives is the low modulation depth of the grating due to the random diffusion of electrons. This entails a low sensitivity.

5.9   Research directions

The search for more sensitive holographic recording media continues. Perhaps, this will lead to the use of dynamic holograms in those materials that have no storage characteristics. There are a number of thermo-optic materials with much higher sensitivity than those discussed earlier, such as the liquid crystals. Meanwhile, a number of laboratories are becoming proficient in dichromated gelatin usage. Moreover, there are continuing advances in reducing noise and increasing cycling capability of thermoplastics, novel photorefractive crystal synthesis, and the possibility of wider use of photopolymers now that they are available as a commercial product.

CHAPTER 6
SYSTEM DEVELOPMENTS

6.1 Introduction

While conventional holographic pattern recognition systems can identify a target rapidly by matching it to information stored in either a holographic template (FPC) or a frame store (JTC), they suffer a basic limitation in that the target images must match the template or frame store image exactly. A significant amount of progress has been made in generalizing the pattern matching capability of the memory correlator (FPC), and this will be discussed from the point of view of pre-processing (Section 6.3), optimized filtering (Section 6.4) and post-processing operations (Section 6.5). An important factor for the first two categories has been the development of computer-generated holograms (Section 6.2). The concluding section of this chapter treats some novel system developments that represent more radical departures from the two archetypal systems discussed in Chapter 3.

6.2 Computer-generated holograms

The holograms that are employed in the basic correlator systems are fabricated optically, using extended wavefronts from a laser source. Several methods for extending the application of these systems, in particular the matched filter correlator, require holograms that cannot be fabricated by optical means. The fabrication techniques and methodologies of these holograms are described in the following sections. The amplitude and phase pattern to be recorded on the hologram is available as a mathematical function only. Nevertheless, in comparison with conventional holography, it will be referred to as the object beam.

6.2.1   Fabrication techniques

The first computer-generated hologram (CGH) was hand-drawn [133] (Figure 6.1(a)). A natural extension of this was to employ a computer plotter. An important early example of this technique was the generation of a 64×64 pixel hologram with 15×15 quantization levels per pixel (or hologram cell) [134]. Due to the coarseness of the stepping increment of the pen and the width of the stroke, the dimensions of the holograms were 25×25 cm^2. Therefore, a photoreduction step is important. A demagnification of between 100 and 400:1 increased the resolution and ensured an adequate separation of the diffracted beam from undiffracted light. The **space bandwidth product (SBWP)** of this hologram is $(64 \times 15)^2$; that is, about 10^6. There is experimental evidence that this is adequate for pattern recognition. Specifically, the filters used in the correlator described in [135], were prepared by a two-dimensional laser-scanning system that generated holograms of similar SBWP [136]. Moreover, the SLMs used in correlators have lower SBWPs than this.

However, two hologram writers of higher quality have been developed. The Aerodyne writer [137] composes the hologram on a photographic plate from a number of sub-holograms, which are accurately 'stitched' together using an X/Y locator under microcomputer control. The sub-holograms are formed by demagnification of a cathode ray tube (CRT) picture. The Optronics 1600 film writer is a commercial product. Here, an LED scans across a photographic film that is mounted on a rotating drum. Photographic emulsion has sufficient dynamic range for accurate grey level coding. Both of the above systems achieve SBWPs of 10^8.

There is a growing interest in the application of e-beam pattern generators to hologram writing [138, 139]. The e-beam spot size is about 0.1 μm, and high SBWPs can be achieved. Some of the SBWP is allocated to the spatial coding of grey levels, since this procedure generates binary holograms. The coding techniques for plotter and e-beam holograms are discussed in the next section.

6.2.2   Methodologies

The binary amplitude hologram employs opaque and transparent elementary areas, and codes the amplitude of the reconstructed wave in terms of the size

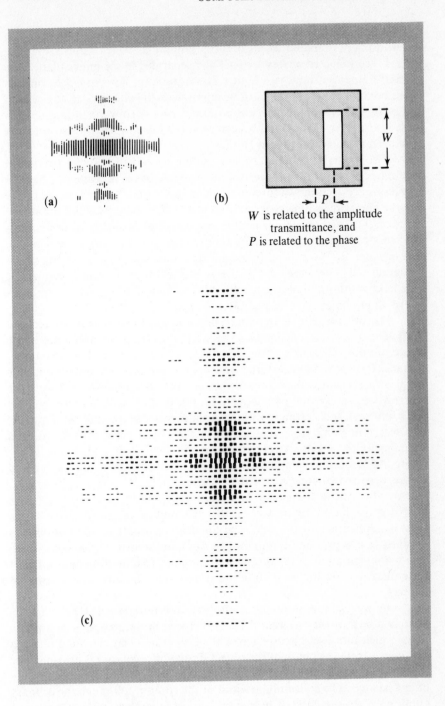

(a)

(b)

W is related to the amplitude
transmittance, and
P is related to the phase

(c)

Figure 6.1   Types of computer-generated hologram (I).

of the transparent area and the phase in terms of its relative position. It is conventionally prepared as an off-axis hologram, which implies that the several reconstructed beams are spatially separated in the image plane. The off-axis hologram employs a higher SBWP than the corresponding on-axis form, because a fine grating must be imposed on the object beam so that off-axis beam diffraction occurs. Nevertheless, it is worthwhile in that on-axis noise is removed. (This is not necessary in the binary phase holograms that have been recently introduced [140].)

The spatial frequency of the grating should exceed the maximum spatial frequency of the object by a further 50% of the maximum, when the grey levels are accurately represented in the hologram. The reason for this is that the binary recording generates so-called 'false' images, which are superposed on the 'true' images. These false images result from higher order auto- and cross-correlations and, when they are superposed on the on-axis image, they broaden it. The grating frequency determines the repeat spacing of the hologram cell. The remainder of the SBWP is disposed towards coding the grey level within the hologram cell. It is the aim of advanced coding techniques to minimize the effect of false images.

Historically, the first coding technique was the **detour phase method** [133]. The hologram is divided into cells and the object beam sampled at the centre of each cell. The recording is made so that each cell has zero transmittance, except for an aperture whose area is proportional to the amplitude of the object beam at the centre of the cell, and which is displaced from the centre by an amount corresponding to the phase of the sampled beam (Figure 6.1(b) and (c)). A disadvantage of this technique is that the aperture is located at a different point from that at which the object beam is sampled, and sampling errors result. A refinement of this method is that of Lee [141], where the function is sampled at four equidistant points within the cell and aperture windows are generated at these points. A further refinement, namely the **Allebach–Keagan hologram** [142], samples the object wave at every resolution point within the cell and a variable binary threshold is applied across the cell. The quadrature aspect of the sampling is retained, since groups of four points are thresholded at the same level. The spatial variation of the threshold is designed to minimize the overlap of false images from higher diffraction orders into the diffraction order of interest.

An alternative approach is the **Lee interferogram** [141]. A mathematical model of the 'reference' beam is stored in the computer as a phase term, which increases linearly across the hologram. This reference phase is subtracted from the phase of the object beam and a contour is drawn where this difference is equal to an odd multiple of π radians. The amplitude of the object beam can be coded in the width of the contour, although the primary application for this type of hologram is to encode phase-only information (Figure 6.2(a)). In the latter case, a contour width of one-half the fringe spacing will ensure a maximum diffraction efficiency of 10%. If, further, the

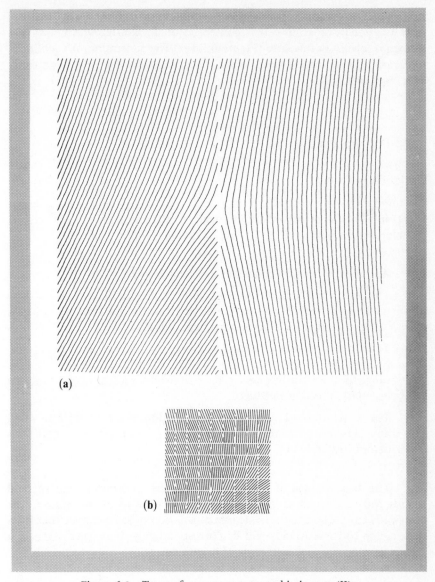

(a)

(b)

Figure 6.2   Types of computer-generated hologram (II).

hologram is subsequently bleached, the resulting phase hologram gives a diffraction efficiency close to 40%.

A theoretical analysis of reconstruction errors in terms of false images is presented in [143]. This is the relevant form of analysis for the correlator system. An alternative form of analysis, which quantifies the mean square error in the reconstruction on a pixel-by-pixel basis [144, 145], is important when the cosmetic quality of the reconstruction is important.

Finally, a **scanning interferometric pattern (SIP)** system was described in [136]. Each hologram cell is composed of an interferogram, which is formed optically in this case (Figure 6.2(b)). The generation of each interferogram and its location are under microcomputer control via galvanometric scanners.

6.3   Pre-processing

6.3.1   Phase coding

The input data can be encoded as phase information by complex exponentiation [146]. This is performed automatically by the phase-only SLMs, such as the micromechanical devices. Several advantages follow from this.

- A higher diffraction efficiency can be achieved.

- The energy in the undiffracted beam can be significantly reduced (in the hypothetical case of the resultant phasor of the sum of the pixels being zero, there will be no zero-order beam).

- The Fourier plane spectrum is more delocalized than the corresponding amplitude case; this eases the requirements on the dynamic range for the recording device and, in the ideal case, a sharp δ-function correlation peak is produced.

- The correlation is highly resistant to random noise on the inputs and any bias level difference between them. The practical benefit was demonstrated in [147].

The disadvantage of a delocalized Fourier spectrum is that spectral islands will be formed at larger distances from the focal spot than in the amplitude case. Therefore, the degree of rotation or scale change that loses the overlap of these islands will be correspondingly diminished. Hence, a greater intolerance to these forms of misalignment.

Similar advantages are gained by the use of a **phase mask** placed downline and close to the input. The mathematical form of the phase mask can be designed to increase the light throughput of the system [148]. Alternatively, it can be designed to increase the parallelism of the system, as in the coded phase processor [149]. Here, the phase mask is employed in recording a number of templates on a single recording device. For each new input, the mask is translated by a known distance, and this uniquely codes each template in the Fourier plane. The disadvantage in the use of phase masks is that spatial invariance is lost, and the system is intolerant to translation of the object in the input scene.

6.3.2 Co-ordinate transforms

In those cases where the scale/orientation of the object is altered between the formation of the template and the object's reappearance in the scene, a system invariant to these changes must be developed. The scale/orientation invariance is generated by co-ordinate transformations on the input plane and is created either opto-mechanically, electronically or with the assistance of CGHs.

The intensity of the correlation signal from an unmodified Vander Lugt correlator can be halved by either a 0.5% scale change or a 0.2° rotation of the object, as a worst-case situation [150]. For modest scale changes (up to 20%), a scaling correlator configuration [151] can be adopted. Here, the input device is located in the converging light beam after the first Fourier transform lens, rather than in the front focal plane. This configuration is advantageously applied to scale the Fourier transform when the wavelength of the read beam differs from that employed in recording the template. To rotate the object beam, the opto-mechanical option is a prism that can be rotated. A number of alternative prisms, of which the Dove prism is an example, have been evaluated theoretically in [152]. There is a significant possibility of beam wander when these are inserted and rotated in the coherent part of the system; for example, between the input device and the Fourier transform lens. This would cause the misalignment of the Fourier spectra. However, this problem is avoided if the prism is placed on the incoherent side of an OASLM. This arrangement was adopted in the correlator described in the appendix, where it was observed that the prism can cause distortion of the pattern.

In those cases where the input device is optically addressed from a CRT, the deflection coils of the CRT can be controlled by digital/analogue or analogue circuits to generate scaling and/or rotation [40]. Alternatively, these functions can be incorporated into a 'smart' SLM, such as the Hamamatsu microchannel SLM, which achieves $\pm 30\%$ zooming ratio in addition to a full 360° rotational capability [153].

In those instances where tracking is not desired, the input plane co-ordinates can be assigned to the radial and orientational co-ordinates, (r, Θ). If a camera is modified to scan in successive concentric circles, the result is termed a **polar camera** [154]. The video signal is connected to either a monitor, a scanning e-beam or an acousto-optic modulator for interface to the SLM [155]. If no further transformation is applied to the video signal, the correlation generated will be rotationally invariant for rotations about the centre defined by the video camera. Two correlation spots are formed, separated by the equivalent of 2π radians on the correlation plane axis. These must be summed to provide the correlation corresponding to the full object. To include scale invariance in this system, the r-axis must be transformed to a ln r-axis. This is implemented electronically by placing a logarithmic module on, for example, the current to the deflector coils of the monitor. The scaling factor can then be recovered from the correlation plane. The logarithmic scaling of the input co-ordinates, in conjunction with the Fourier transformation, is known as the **Mellin transform**.

The ln r-Θ transform has also been generated using a CGH [156] (Figure 6.2(a)). The hologram is a Lee interferogram placed adjacent to the input transparency, and the transformed version of the input appears in the focal plane of a Fourier transform lens. The transformation was performed on the incoherent side of an optically addressed light valve. However, an Ar$^+$ laser was employed because of the phase coherence required for the holographic transformation.

In addition to the loss of spatial invariance in a co-ordinate transformed correlator, there is an increase in the SBWP required to represent the image [157]. In other words, a greater number of resolution cells, perhaps an order of magnitude more, are required to maintain the spatial resolution of the image.

Multi-channel one-dimensional signals, for example radar, can be applied to the input SLM on a one-channel-per-line basis [158] or with raster scanning [159]. The former approach can result in faster frame rates for the input device where the speed is limited by the data rate. The optical system is configured to generate the one-dimensional transforms of each line, preserving the vertical position of each line in the process. The matched filter is a one-dimensional transform replicated vertically for each line, and the correlation plane is a vertical sequence of one-dimensional correlation products. The raster scanning must be adopted when the SBWP of the date exceeds that of a line of the SLM [160]. A falling raster, for example on a TV monitor, is to be preferred to a non-falling raster to exclude the possibility of intermodulation effects between the diffraction pattern of the rectangular SLM aperture and the Fourier spectrum of the signal [161].

6.3.3 Point transforms

The image, as viewed, is not always optimum for recognition in the optical correlator. For example, there may be a higher SNR of the correlation peak if a line drawing of the edges of the object were used, both for the template and scene information. The pre-processing operations that are involved have been borrowed from digital image processing, where the emphasis has been on improving the cosmetic quality of the image. In addition, the treatment of signal-dependent noise is relevant here. Point transforms can be described as mathematical operations on the pixel value, which may or may not include the values of neighbouring pixels.

The example of edge definition can be enacted in, at least, two different ways: high-pass filtering or by applying a gradient operator. High-pass filtering is generally implemented in the frequency plane by blocking the low-frequency components. This increases the sensitivity of the correlator to scale and rotation changes. In addition, it reduces the light intensity. In contrast, the gradient operator redistributes the light intensity to the contour lines in the object. There is more energy available at the high spatial frequencies, allowing larger fringe modulation in the Fourier plane hologram, larger diffraction efficiency and more intensity in the correlation spot. These observations have been confirmed experimentally in [162]. When noise is present, the selection of the optimal differential operator is more involved [163].

The implementation of edge enhancement relies either on SLMs with this functionality or on CGHs. The Hamamatsu MSLM includes edge enhancement as part of its repertoire of functions, while the differentiating SLM (DSLM) [164] generates contours by using a homeotropically aligned liquid crystal in a BSO LCLV. When a CGH is used, the edge enhancement function is conveniently represented as a Fourier transform and placed in the frequency plane [165]. Due to the limited depth of focus of the Fourier transform lens, it may be more convenient to place the point transform, only, in the frequency plane and image this on to a further frequency plane where the matched filter is located.

A more elementary transform is the **thresholding operation**. When this is implemented at the device level (that is, using a binary SLM), faster framing speeds are possible, and the uniformity of the threshold across the device, which is important for accurate grey scale production, is no longer a stringent requirement. However, at the system level, a number of other pre-processing operations, such as histogram shaping, must be implemented so that the binary image is an accurate representation of the object. This was performed in [166], where the image was further processed by an alternative optical pattern recognition technique. For cluttered or noisy scenes, grey level input is preferred. In those cases where the noise is signal dependent, a non-linear grey scale is appropriate [167]. Finally, it has been shown by computer simulation [168] that the discrimination gained in a correlator can be improved by varying the grey scale coding; for example, using a logarithmic grey scale.

6.4 Optimized filtering

6.4.1 Introduction

The basic Vander Lugt correlator employs a matched filter in the frequency plane. A matched filter is one for which the transfer function is the complex conjugate of the spectrum of the signal [8]. It is the optimum filter for signal identification in 'white' noise. When the noise has a spatial frequency dependence, or is signal dependent, then the pre-processing operations are relevant. When the recognition task is more complex – for example, identification of a class of objects or discrimination between a finite number of similar objects – then techniques from statistical pattern recognition

(Section 6.4.2) or the use of synthetic discriminant functions (Section 6.4.3) must be considered. Alternatively, the problem of scale/orientational invariance could be tackled at the filter stage, either by using multiplexed filters (Section 6.4.4) or, in the case of orientational invariance, using circular harmonic filters (Section 6.4.5).

6.4.2   Statistical pattern recognition

The pixels of a two-dimensional image are ordered in a raster fashion as a one-dimensional vector. Due to the variability of the image (for example, scale, rotation, distortion, class), this is considered a random vector with an associated probability distribution. The covariance matrix of this distribution is treated according to the methods of **statistical pattern recognition theory**.

If the eigenvectors of the covariance matrix are calculated, then it is commonly the case that a small number of these are associated with large eigenvalues. These are termed 'dominant' eigenvectors and can be used to characterize the image. For example, if these vectors were reordered into a set of two-dimensional images, and a multiplexed filter of their Fourier transforms produced, then this filter could be used in the memory correlator for the recognition of all images within the class defined by the probability distribution. This is termed 'intra-class' recognition, and the eigenvector expansion is the discrete version of the **Karhunen–Loeve (KL) expansion**. The calculation of eigenvectors is performed 'off-line' on a computer, and a training set of images defines the probability distribution. The eigenvector expansion is a best fit to the image set in a 'mean squares' sense. The mean square deviation of the expansion from the image set is equal to the sum of the eigenvalues of the vectors omitted from the expansion [169]. Hence, the importance of the 'dominant' eigenvectors. Two examples of the practical application of this expansion [170, 171] employ these techniques in the Fourier plane rather than the image plane.

The KL expansion provides optimal 'intra-class' recognition. However, a further elaboration is required when the discrimination between two object classes is required ('inter-class' discrimination). In the **Fukunaga–Koontz (FK) transformation**, the covariance matrices for each class are simultaneously diagonalized by the same transformation. The existence of such a transformation is demonstrated in [172]. Moreover, it is shown that the dominant eigenvectors of one class are associated with the smallest eigenvalues in the second class, and vice versa. This implies that efficient discrimination can be achieved when a filter composed of the Fourier transforms of the dominant eigenvectors is employed. A practical realization of this, using phase coding to multiplex the Fourier transforms, is detailed in [172]. Two further feature extraction techniques, which are applicable when the number of object classes exceeds two, are described in [173, 174].

Alternatively, the multi-class recognition problem can be tackled by composing a filter that generates a binary-coded correlation plane response [175]. (The concept of binary coding in the correlation plane, which reduces the dimensionality of the classes, originated in the literature in [176].) Finally, a **generalized matched filter (GMF)** can be composed for multi-class discrimination and, in addition, to correct for space variance due to non-ideal Fourier transform lenses [177, 178].

6.4.3   Synthetic discriminant functions

All the statistical techniques that have been described require an appropriate mathematical calculation to determine a basis function set for the fabrication of the filter. For example, the dominant eigenvectors of the covariance matrix must be determined in the KL expansion. In contrast, the **synthetic discriminant functions (SDFs)** [179] use the image set itself as basis functions, and the weight of each basis function in the filter is determined by inverting the covariance matrix. Specifically, the weights form a vector that is given by the product of the inverse of the correlation matrix with a control vector. The control vector is determined by the recognition task in hand. For example, if it is a requirement that every image in the set should produce a correlation peak of equal intensity, then the control vector is a sequence of 1s; if the images occurring in the training set are to remain invisible to the correlator, then 0s are inserted in the control vector in the appropriate positions, etc.

The main virtue of this approach is the reduced computational complexity of filter fabrication. However, good judgement is necessary to determine the size and composition of the training set. Two systematic selection procedures are detailed in [180].

The practical realizations of this approach have been limited to computer simulations. For example, contrast reversed silhouettes of ships [181], infra-red images of tanks [182] and laboratory images of tanks [183]. A refined SDF approach, which reduces the level of the side lobes in the neighbourhood of the correlation peak, by recording extra (shifted) versions of each image of the training set, has been simulated and is described in [184].

6.4.4   Multiplexed filters

The processing power of the memory correlator can be increased by recording more filter functions at the frequency plane. These can be either spatially or frequency multiplexed, or a combination of the two.

When each hologram is recorded at a separate location, the composite hologram is said to be **spatially multiplexed** or **block oriented**. This might be achieved by a deflection system on the beam that interrogates the input SLM, so that a different angle of incidence is associated with each input template. However, the Fourier transform lens is not designed for low aberration at large field angles, with the consequence that off-axis filter functions exhibit some space variance. However, a multiple focus Fourier transform lens could be fabricated as a CGH and optimized for low aberration at each focal point. This is called a **multi-focus hololens**, and was originally suggested for this application in [185]. A 25-focus hololens has been fabricated in dichromated gelatin [186]. The 25 filter functions were recorded sequentially, using the same reference beam, by employing a mask at the filter plane. A conventional Fourier transform lens is used in the second stage of the correlator (Figure 6.3). This will co-locate the correlation spots from each filter function, and these will add coherently with phase factors determined by the separation of the function in the filter plane. It is important, therefore, that the filter functions are quasi-orthogonal, with small cross-correlations, so that the intensity of the correlation spot is not attenuated by destructive interference. Alternatively, a defocussed correlation plane can be used where the correlation spots are spatially separated. An alternative method for generating the 25 filter locations is to place a contact screen at the input plane [187]. The contact screen is a close approximation to the Fourier transform of a 5×5 array of δ-functions. However, this places the same demands on the Fourier transform lens as the beam deflection method mentioned previously. Finally, the density of spectral islands in the filter plane can be augmented by close packing and recording one-half, only, of symmetrical spectra [188].

A **frequency multiplexed** hologram is composed by recording each input with the reference wave at a new angle of incidence. The angular selectivity of each hologram determines the number of separate angles of incidence that can be used, and in the thick holographic materials this angular selectivity is sharp. On the face of it, it would seem that a large number of recordings could be multiplexed. However, shot noise considerations set a limit to the minimum modulation depth of each recording [189], and the total modulation depth is limited by the dynamic range of the material. Moreover, in the photorefractive crystals, the subsequent recordings will abstract electrons from the initial recording and decrease its modulation depth. In addition, complexity is added to the system design to generate the range of incident angles and the consequent spatial separation of the correlation planes corresponding to each recording. Consequently, the practical application of this technique has been limited to low-level multiplexing. Typical numbers indicate that the angle of incidence should be incremented by 10° for each recording on photographic plate [190]. The corresponding wavelength selectivity of thick holograms has not been exploited in this context. If the laser could be tuned, then a constant reference beam angle and correlation plane could be used. The wavelength should be incremented by approximately 100 Å for a recording medium of thickness 1 mm [190].

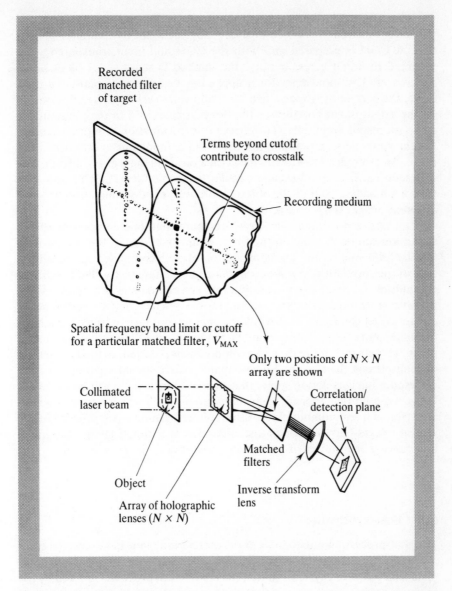

Figure 6.3 A spatially multiplexed matched filter image correlator. (Reproduced by kind permission of Grumman.)

6.4.5 Circular harmonic filters

One approach to rotation-invariant recognition is to use a filter that is matched to one of the circular harmonic expansion components of the target [191]. The **circular harmonic expansion** is a series expansion of the target, expressed as a polar function, in terms of the sines and cosines of multiples of the polar angle. The optimal components of the expansion and a centre for the target function in polar co-ordinates are calculated by computer simulation. A CGH is prepared and both the CGH and input transparency are mounted in liquid gates, because the method is sensitive to small phase differences. Threshold detection is applied at the correlation plane. Furthermore, the correlator is space invariant, allowing tracking. The information on the extent of the rotation of the target is contained in the phase of the correlation spot amplitude. To retrieve this information, a more elaborate system would be required, perhaps involving homodyning at the correlation plane. An example of this technique at the Fourier plane is given in [192]. The diffraction efficiency of a scalar circular harmonic filter (CHF) is less than that of a matched filter of the object. Moreover, the discrimination between different images is less sharp.

There is no simple way in which more than one component of the expansion can be included in the filter. Simple addition of the components has the following result. The contribution of each component to the amplitude of the correlation spot is accompanied by a phase factor that is a different multiple of the degree of rotation for each component. Therefore, some loss of correlation peak intensity could result from destructive interference at certain target rotations. This would be counter-productive, since the aim of including more components would be to increase the SNR at the correlation plane. Therefore, if more than one component is required, so too is a method of multiplexing them in the Fourier plane to give spatial separation of the corresponding correlation spots; that is, spatial invariance will be forfeited. However, a unified approach has been developed in which a filter is generated from a linear combination of the circular harmonic components of the several images between which discrimination is required [193]. Rotational invariance is the subject of much active research at the present time.

6.5   Post-processing

The post-processing possibilities in the correlation plane have received comparatively little attention. In many cases, the correlator is viewed as a complete data reduction system, so that the recognition process is marked by the presence or absence of a correlation spot using a threshold detection scheme. A number of the refinements that have been discussed are directed towards sharpening this spot spatially to improve the SNR; for example, the use of phase input information. However, in the work of Merkle [194], it is demonstrated by computer simulation that when further electronic analysis is performed on the shape of the correlation peak, there are beneficial effects with regard to the discrimination.

The correlation peak is transferred to an image memory via a fast analogue-to-digital converter. In parallel, the signal is transferred to a second image memory via a thresholding device. The first memory stores a grey scale image of the peak, which is further processed to provide a number of features. The most relevant of these, for the chosen task of character recognition, are histograms of grey level slopes and curvatures. The binary image in the second memory provides information on the contour features. The histograms and contour features improve the tolerance of the system to rotational and scale misalignments. The figures quoted are exceptional – for example, up to 30° rotation or 30–40% scaling – and if they are applicable to the practical implementation, then a powerful system has been developed. In a real-time application, consideration would need to be given to the speed at which the relevant post-processing operations could be performed.

6.6   Novel systems

The conventional beam geometry in the JTC was given in Figure 3.6. The recording is interrogated from the left-hand side with collimated light at a wavelength that does not erase the hologram, or erases it very slowly. If the 'read' wavelength is the same as the 'write' wavelength, and it is incident from the right-hand side and co-linear with one of the 'write' beams (Figure 6.4), then a correlation signal can be generated by **degenerate four-wave mixing** [195]. This effect is only applicable to real-time recording materials of the monolithic type and, preferentially, those that exhibit a diffusive non-linearity. The diffusive non-linearity (for example, that found in photo-refractives) allows independent optimization of the three beam intensities [196]. Correlation has been demonstrated experimentally using lithium tantalate [197] and BSO [198]. An advantage of this system is that aberrations are minimized because the wavelength of reconstruction is the same as the write wavelength. A disadvantage is that the non-linear gain of the material must remain low to avoid harmonic distortion. However, the small optical non-linearity of current materials satisfies this criterion.

The beam geometry of the JTC is also modified in the **dual-axis correlator** [128] (Figure 6.5). The cost of the Fourier transform lens increases with the aperture of the lens. To reduce cost, two smaller lenses are employed for the two signal beams. Furthermore, to ensure that the Fourier transforms are superposed correctly, the optic axes of the two lenses must intersect at the frequency plane. The disadvantage of this is that, whereas the multiplication of low frequency components is satisfactory, a phase delay, which increases with the frequency, is introduced for the higher spatial frequencies. This limits the SBWP of the system.

The **transposed processor** [199] is a memory correlator with the scene composing the filter function and the template imposed on the interrogating beam. The main advantage of this system is the good noise rejection. Noise is associated with the scene rather than the template; it has a high dynamic range with a peak at low spatial frequencies. The non-linearities associated

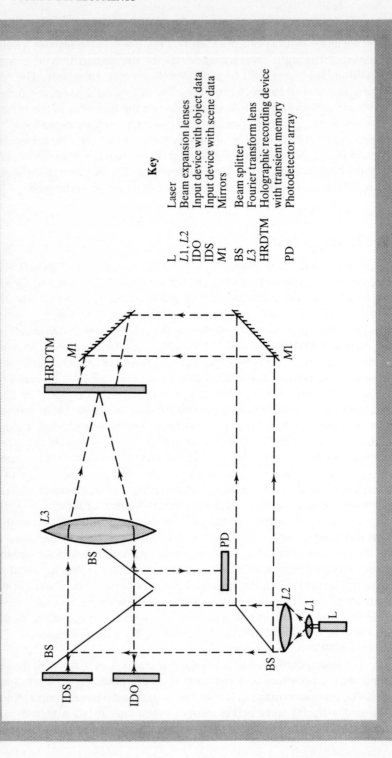

Key

L	Laser
L1, L2	Beam expansion lenses
IDO	Input device with object data
IDS	Input device with scene data
M1	Mirrors
BS	Beam splitter
L3	Fourier transform lens
HRDTM	Holographic recording device with transient memory
PD	Photodetector array

Figure 6.4 System layout for degenerate four-wave mixing correlator.

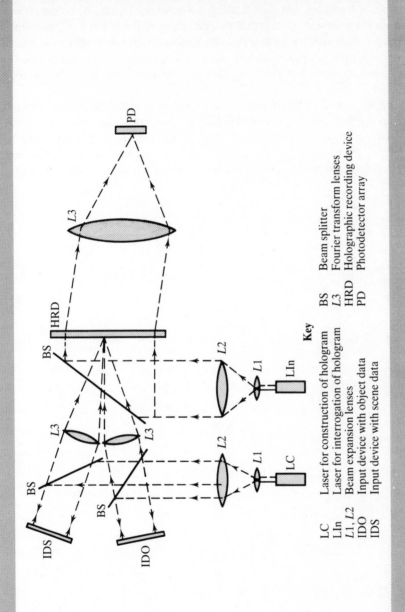

Figure 6.5 System layout for dual-axis correlator.

Key

LC   Laser for construction of hologram   BS   Beam splitter
LIn   Laser for interrogation of hologram $L3$ Fourier transform lenses
$L1, L2$ Beam expansion lenses   HRD   Holographic recording device
IDO   Input device with object data   PD   Photodetector array
IDS   Input device with scene data

with holographic emulsion reduce the recorded noise. Moreover, the mathematical form of the non-linearity is such that it creates a filter of optimum noise rejection quality. Since saturation is a common feature of holographic recording materials, it is likely that similar arguments will hold for real-time materials. A secondary advantage of this system is that the template function is more amenable to modification, such as scaling/rotation, etc. It is this system geometry that has been employed in the correlator described in the appendix.

Finally, a method of optical processing to recognize objects in an extended depth of field is presented in [200]. The Fourier transform is imaged on to the recording medium via a **Fabry Perot etalon**, which generates a multiplicity of templates. These correspond to a succession of objects along the optic axis separated by a distance of $2d$, where d is the gap spacing of the etalon.

CHAPTER 7
APPLICATIONS AND ALTERNATIVES

7.1   Introduction

The approach to optical correlation that has been described would be widely applied if cheap devices were commercially available. However, this field of technology, at present, lacks an application where this approach is the only solution, and which will 'drive the technology'. An idea of areas where this technology can be profitably applied is given in Section 7.2. The increasing importance of image processing is demonstrated by the development of specialist electronic hardware, which is perhaps better viewed as another building block in this field rather than competition for optical hardware. However, in Section 7.3, the electronic systems overlap with optical correlators is described and performance figures given for comparison.

7.2   Application areas

The systems that have been described in the foregoing chapters are optimal for template matching. They are most appropriate in those cases where high

95

noise rejection, high speed, low cost or a compact system is required. The natural, as opposed to man-made, environment poses significant noise problems, particularly in the areas of missile guidance, vehicle guidance, aerial photometry and synthetic aperture radar (SAR). Optical correlators are being tested on missiles in the US, although a significant research effort will be required to make these systems rugged. Currently, the aerial recon-naissance satellites collect information in two forms, electronic SAR data and optical multi-spectral imagery/aerial photography. In the 1960s and 1970s, there was a large research effort in optical SAR processing. A spatially encoded optical beam is a natural representation of the microwave beam, and the co-ordinate transformations that are required for reconstruction can be performed by lenses. In addition, the high dynamic range of the radar returns would favour an analogue system, such as the optical correlator. However, the input device for experimental SAR systems never progressed beyond the photographic transparency. Electronic processing, using array processors, is currently favoured. For the photographic data, which has a lower resolution, optical techniques prevail, and an example of a complete system design in this respect is given in [201].

The speed advantage of the optical system is due to the highly parallel nature of the computation. In certain cases, such as document reading, it is quite acceptable to have a slow electronic system operating on a 24-hour basis. However, in visual inspection, the processing time can limit the throughput of the production line. In particular, a commercial holographic system has recently been developed for wafer inspection in the semiconductor industry [202]. It is claimed that sub-micron size defects can be found in a 150 mm wafer, and the complete wafer can be inspected within 30 minutes. The image input into the system is the direct reflection of coherent light from the surface of the wafer. A hologram is formed close to the Fourier plane of the image, and a reconstruction of the hologram is sufficient for detecting defects. The recording material used is photographic emulsion, and it is not difficult to envisage faster processing speeds with real-time devices. There is a considerable advantage when the input image is received directly from the object.

The final attributes of optics, low cost and compactness go together to a certain extent. The major expense in contemporary systems is the input SLM. However, when this item is produced in volume, the major expense will be the optical system assembly. A 'glass block' correlator [52], where the light paths are confined within a superstructure of prisms, spacers and beam splitters, and the components are mounted on the external facets, is com-pact and readily visualized as a mass produced item. The power consump-tion is significantly less than electronic counterparts, making these systems prime candidates for spacecraft applications, which include data analysis, control of docking manoeuvres and navigation with respect to the fixed stars [203].

7.3   Alternative correlators

For applications where a correlation is the best detection strategy, and where the number of pixels in the image is large, digital electronic hardware is slow. A typical speed for a one-dimensional Fourier transform on a mainframe computer is about 100 ms for a 1024-point Fast Fourier Transform (FFT), while a more modestly sized minicomputer will take an order of magnitude longer. The two-dimensional transform, 1024×1024, will take three orders of magnitude longer.

There have been several alternative approaches to improving the speed of electronics. There is a class of array processors, of the von Neumann type machines, that have been optimized for high-speed calculations of particular arithmetic functions. Such processors will perform the two-dimensional 1024×1024 transform on the order of seconds [204]. They are available as plug-in boards for mini/mainframe computers. The development of parallel array processors, such as the DAP (ICL) and MPP (NASA–Goodyear), leads to a decrease in the processing time of the number of PEs, which are arranged in parallel. In these architectures, nearest neighbour transfers can take place between the PEs, but for the Fourier transform, which requires a global connectivity between PEs, a reconfigurable network routes the data between successive passes through the array. The parallel array processors are bulky development machines at present, but VLSI implementations are envisaged. A third resolution is to connect together dedicated signal processing chips; the processing power is again of the order of seconds for two-dimensional 512×512 transforms [204]. However, the cost is significantly reduced with respect to the array processor.

When specific VLSI designs are considered, there are schemes for performing the correlation directly, using either systolic or wavefront processing [205]. The more mature technology is **systolic processing** in which the PEs are configured in a pipeline. Suppose that the number of PEs is equal to the number of pixels in the template. The pixels of both the scene and the template are clocked through the PEs in parallel, but at different speeds. The multiplication and summation proceed as the data flows through the array, so that the output of the processor during any one clock cycle is a point in the correlation plane. Successive points are output during the following clock cycles. The more speculative **wavefront processing** is based on asynchronous computing. The master clock is removed because clock skew is a problem in high-speed VLSI circuits. In the wavefront array, it is the arrival of data at the PE that is the signal for processing to commence.

7.4   Concluding remarks

The main thrust of research in this area is directed towards low-cost, compact systems. Of central importance is a cheap SLM with more than 10^4 pixels (or resolution elements) in an area of less than 15 cm². Video frame rates will allow the tracking of slow-moving objects, and analogue operation is preferred. For the dedicated correlator, the supply of and fabrication techniques for the CGHs should improve. For more flexible systems, an inexpensive recording material is awaited. Perhaps, this will be one of the non-linear media, which are now being studied. The final success of these systems will rest with the development of devices that are compatible with semiconductor lasers.

CONSTRUCTION OF A DEMONSTRATOR OPTICAL CORRELATOR

A1.1 Introduction

The author has been part of a collaborative program concerned with the development of SLMs and holographic recording devices, for a period of three years, between 1983 and 1986. The programme was sponsored by the Department of Trade and Industry, under the JOERS initiative. Part of this work has involved the construction of a demonstrator optical correlator. This will be described here to make explicit some of the practical problems involved.

A1.2 System design

The system chosen was based on the transposed processor concept, which was mentioned at the end of Chapter 6. A hologram is made of the scene and interrogated with a template beam. This arrangement facilitates a rotationally invariant recognition system, since the template can be cycled through an adequate number of different orientations of the object. This is particularly appropriate when the template has a much lower space bandwidth product than the scene and a faster SLM can be employed. The system was targeted at the task of recognizing one key in a bunch of several keys. In addition, since the hologram was recorded on a real-time device, the correlator could be multi-tasked without the need to physically replace the hologram.

    The system layout is given in Figure A1.1 and the components used are listed in Table A1.1. One major design aim was to keep the system compact and self-contained, with the exception of the argon laser (Figure A1.2).

    Since the BSO crystal is photosensitive in the green and blue region of the spectrum, and relatively insensitive in the red, it is convenient to use an argon laser for writing and a helium neon (HeNe) laser for reading the

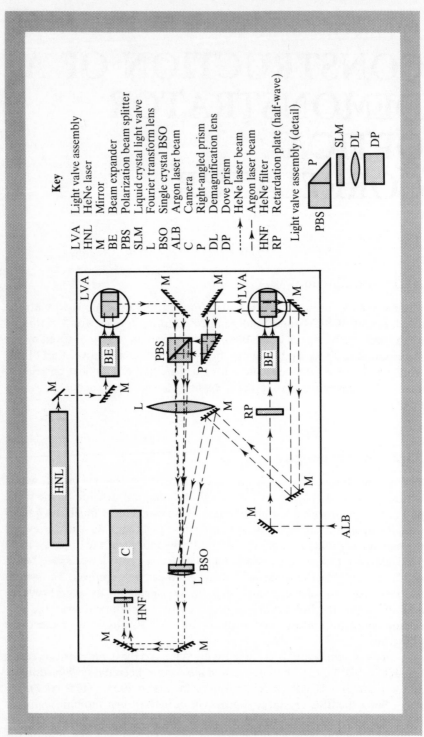

Figure A1.1   System layout of correlator.

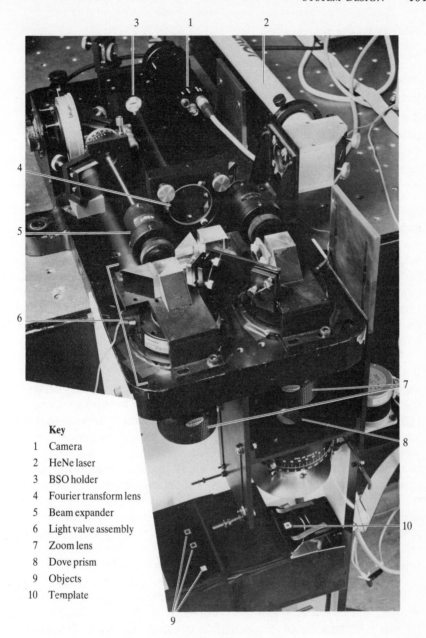

Key

1 Camera
2 HeNe laser
3 BSO holder
4 Fourier transform lens
5 Beam expander
6 Light valve assembly
7 Zoom lens
8 Dove prism
9 Objects
10 Template

Figure A1.2   The optical correlator.

hologram. The 514 nm emission wavelength of the argon laser was selected in preference to the 488 nm line. However, there is not much to choose between these two wavelengths; most of the multi-line argon lasers give a reduced intensity in the blue, but the BSO crystal is more sensitive. A deciding consideration was that the holographic aberrations in the correlation beam depend

Table A1.1   Components.

Item	Supplier	Model
Argon laser	Lexel	75–0.3
HeNe laser	Melles Griot	05 LHP 171
Beam expander ($\times 10$)	Oriel	1590
Polarizing beam splitter	Melles Griot	2609/2610
Fourier transform lens	Melles Griot	01 LAO 238
CCD camera	Pulnix	TM 36 K

on the ratio of the wavelengths of the write and read beams, and, to make this ratio closer to one, the green wavelength was chosen. The power output of the laser, about 100 mW, exceeded the system requirements by an order of magnitude. In this respect, it would have been possible to use a compact, air-cooled argon laser, operating at 488 nm. However, the coherence length of this laser is only a few centimetres (Section 3.5.1), which would have required extra engineering demands to maintain equal reference and object beam paths to this order. Moreover, the large air fan used to cool the laser would have introduced excessive air turbulence and vibration.

A beam height of about 5 cm was found to be the minimum practical. Both laser beams were expanded to a diameter of 1 cm, using compact beam expanders without spatial filtering. The spatial coherence was adequate for the experiments performed. Since it was planned to use optically addressed light valves of the reflective type, the beam path was bent through a right-angle to read the SLMs, which were mounted flat on the optical table and viewed the world below the table. It is conventional practice to pass the read beam through a polarizing beam splitter, so that the object beam reflected from the SLM will be diverted to a different optical path on its return through the beam splitter. This is due to the rotation of the plane of polarization, which is a consequence of the electro-optic effect in the SLM. In addition, the polarizing beam splitter on the argon beam side is used to derive the plane reference beam. The beam ratio of object and reference beam is varied by rotating a half-wave retardation plate in the undilated beam.

The BSO crystal records volume holograms, and the spatial variance can be a major limitation. This effect was minimized by making the angle between the reference and object beams as small as practicable (about 50 mrad). Using a lens of focal length 26 cm, and a 1.2 mm thick crystal, the field of view in the plane of the template SLM was 3 mm. The Bragg angle for the red template beam was close to the angle of incidence of the green object beam, so the two beams were combined using a polarizing beam splitter. Also, the correlation beam was close to the path of the reference beam transmitted by the BSO. This facilitated the alignment of the mirrors which deflected this beam on to the CCD camera. To shorten this beam path, the focussing lens was abutted to the back face of the crystal mount.

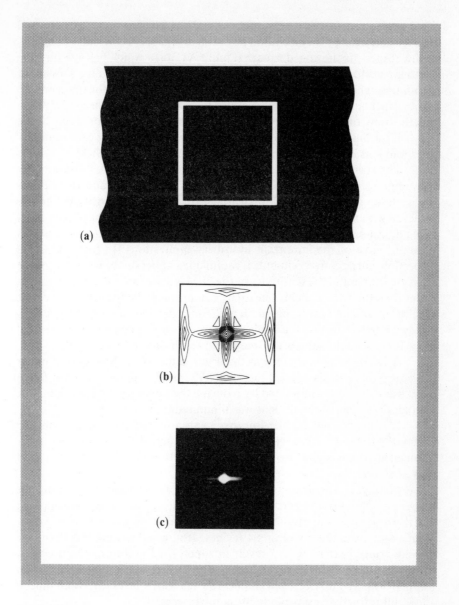

Figure A1.3 Test patterns.

One major experimental difficulty was the alignment of the Fourier transforms of the scene and template on the BSO crystal. In a practical arrangement, the system would be set up using a high laser beam intensity and simple geometric patterns of high contrast on the SLMs. Levelling screws on the template SLM and on the beam steering optics upstream from the lens were sufficient but cumbersome; a better arrangement would have been to have the x- and y-axis, and the skew of the beam as independent adjustments.

The Fourier transforms were brought into coincidence by sight, initially, and then by optimizing the correlation peak height/shape. A convenient pattern, in this respect, is the edged square (Figure A1.3(a)), which has a distinctive Fourier transform (Figure A1.3(b) and (c)). The hologram is erased in about 30 minutes when a HeNe laser beam of 1 mW/cm² is used for the template beam. The Fourier transforms are scaled in accordance with the metric λf, so that the transform of the template would be a magnified version of that of the scene, if the inputs were not scaled accordingly. This scaling is carried out by the zoom lens in the imaging optics on the write side of the SLM.

The stringent writing light conditions required by OASLMs was not fully appreciated at the start of this project. If a zoom lens and Dove prism are included in the write beam, then a sufficient light intensity cannot be achieved with modest light sources and a reflected image of the object. Adequate lighting was achieved only by transmission through screens, and this rules out most of the important industrial applications. In fact, industrial inspection will be convenient only if the imaging optics on the write side of the SLM are simple and the sensitivity of the SLM is about an order of magnitude better than the LCLV. (This sensitivity can probably be reached by the next generation of light valves, based on a silicon photodetector.) A further deficiency related to the use of a Dove prism in a diverging beam is that the focal plane is curved and a distorted image can result on the SLM.

An additional problem was the degradation of the BSO crystal under the large electric fields applied (up to 10 kV/cm). The possibility of a 'flashover' was effectively eliminated by reducing the humidity, and not using the high tension when ambient light was illuminating the crystal.

It is hoped that further improvements will eliminate silver from the electrodes and thus reduce electrode migration across the crystal. A further refinement to the crystal would be the anti-reflection coating of front and back surfaces.

Finally, it was important to use a gated argon beam for writing the hologram. Air currents across the beam paths, or vibration from moving parts, would alter the phase relationship of the scene and reference wavefronts, and move the holographic fringes. If ungated writing was used, the moving fringe pattern would result in superposed gratings, which caused severe fluctuation of the correlation spot intensity. The gating of the beam was performed by an electromechanical switch with a sufficient dwell time to allow full refractive index modulation of the crystal.

In spite of the system deficiencies, a correlation was demonstrated for the object in Figure A1.3(a) by the group at GEC, Hirst. They used the LCLV for both the scene and template SLMs, flash lamp illumination through a screen of the pattern and no Dove prism in the write beam. Subsequently, we demonstrated correlation using BSO LCLVs supplied by British Aerospace.

GLOSSARY

Airy rings   The diffraction pattern produced when light passes through a small pinhole.

Autocorrelation   An image is multiplied by itself on a pixel-by-pixel basis at every possible overlay position.

Beam balance ratio   The ratio of the intensities of object beam and reference beam in holographic recording.

Bragg angle   The angle of incidence of a light beam on a diffraction grating at which the incident and diffracted wave vectors of the light beam form an isosceles triangle with the wave vector of the grating.

Circular harmonic expansion   A series expansion of a polar function in terms of the sines and cosines of multiples of the polar angle.

Coherence length   The distance along a light beam over which the phase varies periodically, without any sharp discontinuities.

Convolution   An image is multiplied by an inverted replica of a second image on a pixel-by-pixel basis at every possible overlay position.

Cross-correlation   An image is multiplied by a second image on a pixel-by-pixel basis at every possible overlay position.

Degenerate four-wave mixing   This occurs in a non-linear medium where four electric wave vectors can be coupled together by a third-order susceptibility.

Detour phase method   A method for coding phase in binary holograms. The phase value is spatially coded by the location of the aperture in the pixel.

Diffraction   The effect of an obstacle on a wave. A patterned screen gives a regular diffraction pattern of light intensity. The light patch that appears in the same position as when there is no screen is called the zero-diffracted order, and the light patch immediately adjacent to this is the first-order diffraction.

Diffraction efficiency   The ratio of first-to-zero order diffracted intensities.

Dual-axis correlator   A particular version of the JTC where separate lenses are used to Fourier transform the object and template images.

Electron-beam (e-beam) address   A method of writing an image by raster scanning an electron beam and depositing charge in selected areas of, for example, an electro-optic crystal.

F#   The F number, or the ratio of the focal length to the aperture of a lens.

Fabry Perot etalon   Two parallel mirrors of low optical absorption that are separated by a gap that is small relative to the coherence length of the light beam.

Feature extraction   The technique of pattern recognition involving the selection of a number of simple characteristics of the pattern.

Fourier hologram   A hologram where the image is recorded as a Fourier transform.

Fourier transform   The plane wave decomposition of an image.

Frequency multiplexed hologram   A composite hologram in which a separate hologram is recorded for each input with the reference wave at a new angle of incidence.

Frequency plane correlator (FPC)   A correlator architecture where one input device and a permanent holographic store are employed.

Fresnel hologram   A hologram formed in the near-field of an image.

Fringe visibility $(I_{max} - I_{min})/(I_{max} + I_{min})$ where I_{max} is the maximum light intensity and I_{min} is the minimum light intensity.

Generalized match filter (GMF)   A filter that is designed for multi-class discrimination by maximizing the difference in the filter output between the selected object and non-selected objects.

Half-wave voltage   The voltage required across an electro-optic crystal to create a path difference of one-half wavelength between the fast and slow axes of the crystal.

Holography   The science of recording complete (amplitude and phase) information relating to an object so that the shape of the object can be perfectly reconstructed from the recording.

Interference   The superposition of two or more light waves at a point.

Interferogram   An interference pattern.

$J_n(x)$ The nth order Bessel function of x.

Joint transform correlator (JTC)   A correlator architecture where two input devices and a refreshable holographic store are employed.

Matched filter   A filter that contains the waveform conjugate to a function or image.

Mellin transform   The Fourier transform of an image that is expressed as a function of logarithmically scaled co-ordinates.

Modulation transfer function (MTF)   The Fourier transform of the response of an SLM, recording medium or lens, etc., to a point source of light. The normalized visibility of fringes is recorded on an SLM or recording medium as a function of their spatial frequency.

MOS transistor (MOST)   Metal-oxide-silicon transistor.

Multi-mode laser   A laser that is configured such that more than one of the longitudinal cavity modes composes the laser beam.

Object beam   The beam that conveys information relating to the template.

Optic axis   The direction through an optical system along which a light beam will suffer minimum aberration.

Paraxial   Close to the optic axis.

Phase mask   A pixellated screen where each pixel can have a different value of phase retardance.

Pockels effect   The birefringence induced by an electric field, which is linear in the electric field. It is measured with high-frequency fields (>10 kHz), so that elasto-optical effects make negligible contribution.

Processing element (PE)   In a computer where the processing power is distributed over a number of locations, such as an array processor, the processing cells are similar and each performs a simple operation. In such cases, they are known as processing elements.

Reconstructed beam   Any beam that appears on irradiation of a hologram.

Reference beam   Plane wave beam used for writing the hologram in the FPC or reading the hologram in the JTC.

Scene beam   The beam that conveys information relating to the scene.

Single-mode laser   A laser that is configured such that only one of the longitudinal cavity modes constitutes the laser beam.

Space bandwidth product (SBWP)   The area divided by the achievable resolution of a device. Effective number of pixels.

Spatial coherence   The degree of phase coherence across an optical wavefront.

Spatial filter   A screen that modifies the cross-sectional profile of an optical wavefront.

Spatial frequency   The reciprocal periodicity of a pattern in space rather than time.

Spatial light modulator (SLM)   An optical device that is capable of altering the direction of a light beam. In this instance, the incident light beam is redirected along the several directions corresponding to the plane wave decomposition of the pattern on the modulator.

Spatial variance   The limitations of an optical system when the object is translated in the object plane.

Spatially multiplexed hologram   A composite hologram in which each individual hologram is recorded in a different spatial position.

Synthetic discriminant function (SDF)   An optimized filter for pattern discrimination that is the Fourier transform of a linear combination of a selection from the set of input images.

Systolic array processor   A regular array of identical PEs with nearest neighbour connections, across which the data items are transferred, so that each individual item passes through a number of PEs between input and output.

Template matching   The technique in pattern recognition where an exact match with one set of stored patterns is sought.

Temporal coherence   The average time between phase discontinuities when a light beam propagates past a point in space. The coherence length divided by the velocity of light.

Thermoplastic   A material that deforms on heating and retains the deformation on subsequent cooling.

Threshold sensitivity   The minimum write beam energy that will impress an image on an OASLM.

Thresholding operation   The conversion of a grey scale image to a binary image.

Transposed processor   A correlator where the filter function is a Fourier transform of the scene, which is interrogated by transforms of templates for search purposes.

Wave vector   A vector, along the direction of the light beam, whose magnitude is the reciprocal of the wavelength, multiplied by 2π.

Wiener–Khinchine theorem   The power spectrum of a function is the Fourier transform of its autocorrelation function.

BIBLIOGRAPHY

[1] Duffieux, P.M., 1983, *The Fourier Transform and its Application to Optics*, Wiley & Sons.

[2] Abu-Mostafa, Y.S. and Psaltis, D., 1987, 'Optical neural computers', *Scientific American*, March, pp. 66–73.

[3] Casasent, D., 1978, *Optical Data Processing*, Springer-Verlag.

[4] Goodman, J.W., 1968, *Introduction to Fourier Optics*, McGraw-Hill.

[5] Lee, S.H., 1981, *Optical Information Processing*, Springer-Verlag.

[6] Gregory, D.A., 1986, 'Real-time pattern recognition using a modified liquid crystal television in a coherent optical correlator', *Appl. Opt.*, **25**, pp. 467–469.

[7] Batchelor, B.G., 1976, *Pattern Recognition*, Plenum Press, pp. 43–64.

[8] Turin, G.L., 1960, 'An introduction to matched filters', *IRE Trans. Inf. Th.*, June, pp. 311–319.

[9] Hassoun, M.H. and Arrathoun, R., 1986, 'Logical signal processing with optically connected logic gates', *Opt. Eng.*, **25**, pp. 56–68.

[10] Soffer, B.H. *et al.*, 1986, 'Associative holographic memory with feedback using phase-conjugate mirrors', *Opt. Lett.*, **11**, pp. 118–120.

[11] Jenkins, B.K. *et al.*, 1984, 'Architectural implications of a digital optical processor', *Appl. Opt.*, **23**, pp. 3465–3474.

[12] Blackburn, H. *et al.*, 1985, 'Advanced algorithms and architectures for voice and image processing', *ESPRIT '84*, Elsevier Science, pp. 159–182.

[13] Yu, F.T.S., 1972, 'Synthesis of an optical-sound spectrograph', *J. Acoust. Soc. Am.*, **51**, pp. 433–438.

[14] Yu, F.T.S. *et al.*, 1985, 'White-light optical speech spectrogram generation', *Appl. Opt.*, **24**, pp. 836–841.

[15] Vienot, F. *et al.*, 1977, 'Sound pattern recognition using optical methods', *Opt. Act.*, **24**, pp. 811–825.

[16] Bridle, J.S. and Moore, R.K., 1984, 'Boltzmann machines for speech pattern processing', *Proc. Inst. Acoust.*, Autumn meeting.

[17] Evangelisti, C.J., 1983, 'Some experiments in the evaluation of a character recognition scanner', *Patt. Rec.*, **16**, pp. 273–287.

[18] Casey, R.G. and Jih, C.R., 1983, 'A processor-based OCR system', *IBM J. Res. Develop.*, **27**, pp. 386–399.

[19] Yoshitake Tsuji and Ko Asai, 1984, 'Character image segmentation', *Proc. SPIE*, **504**, pp. 2–9.

[20] Gabor, D., 1965, 'Character recognition by holography', *Nature*, **208**, pp. 422–423.

[21] Gabor, D., 1948, 'A new microscopic principle', *Nature*, **161**, pp. 777–778.

[22] Leith, E.N. and Upatnieks, J., 1962, 'Reconstructed wavefronts and communication theory', *J. Opt. Soc. Am.*, **52**, pp. 1123–1130.

[23] Casasent, D. and Luu, T., 1978, 'Performance measurement techniques for simple Fourier transform lenses', *Appl. Opt.*, **17**, pp. 2973–2980.

[24] Geary, J. and Peterson, P., 1984, 'Spherical aberration and diffraction derived via Fourier optics', *Opt. Eng.*, **23**, pp. 052–054.

[25] Arecchi, F.T. and Aussenegg, F.R., 1981, *Current Trends in Optics*, Taylor & Francis, pp. 173–188.

[26] Vander Lugt, A.B., 1966, 'Operational notation for the analysis and synthesis of optical data-processing systems', *Proc. IEEE*, **54**, pp. 1055–1063.

[27] Hagler, M.O., 1983, 'Application of Vander Lugt's operational notation to finite aperture lens systems', *Appl. Opt.*, **22**, pp. 768–769.

[28] Bracewell, R., 1965, *The Fourier Transform and its Application*, McGraw-Hill.

[29] Kovasnay, L.S.G. and Arman, A., 1957, 'Optical autocorrelation measurement of two-dimensional random patterns', *Rev. Sci. Instr.*, **28**, pp. 793–797.

[30] Monahan, M. *et al.*, 1977, 'Incoherent optical correlators', *Proc. IEEE*, **65**, pp. 121–129.

[31] Yu, F.T.S., 1983, *Optical Information Processing*, Wiley & Sons.

[32] Vander Lugt, A.B., 1964, 'Signal detection by complex spatial filtering', *IEEE Trans. Inf. Th.*, **10**, pp. 139–145.

[33] Casasent, D. and Furman, A., 1977, 'Optimisation of parameters in matched spatial filter synthesis', *Appl. Opt.*, **16**, pp. 1662–1669.

[34] Vander Lugt, A.B., 1967, 'The effects of small displacements of spatial filters', *Appl. Opt.*, **6**, pp. 1221–1225.

[35] Guenther, B.D. *et al.*, 1979, 'Coherent optical processing: another approach', *IEEE J. Qu. Elect.*, **15**, pp. 1348–1362.

[36] Bage, M.J. and Beddoes, M.P., 1976, 'Lensless matched filter: operating principle, sensitivity to spectrum shift, and third-order holographic aberrations', *Appl. Opt.*, **15**, pp. 2830–2839.

[37] Rau, J.E., 1966, 'Detection of differences in real distributions', *J. Opt. Soc. Am.*, **56**, pp. 1490–1494.

[38] Weaver, C.S. and Goodman, J.W., 1966, 'A technique for optically convoling two functions', *Appl. Opt.*, **5**, pp. 1248–1249.

[39] Wehrenberg, P.J. and Richards, M.J., 1979, 'Effects of wavefront modulator characteristics on joint transform correlator performance', *Proc. SPIE*, **202**, pp. 98–101.

[40] Hester, C.F. and Brown, H.B., 1980, 'Optical joint transform image correlation system', *Proc. SPIE*, **255**, pp. 126–135.

[41] Elkhov, V.A. *et al.*, 1982, 'Effect of coherence of radiation on the form of the output signal in an optical correlator', *Autometriya*, **5**, pp. 60–64.

[42] Zolitarev, A.I. *et al.*, 1982, 'Effect of the spectral characteristics of the radiation of injection lasers on the form of the correlation signal in the Vander Lugt correlator system', *Autometriya*, **5**, pp. 64–69.

[43] Home Dickson, J., 1970, *Optical Instruments and Techniques*, Oriel Press.

[44] Casasent, D. and Luu, T., 1978, 'Phase error model for simple Fourier transform lenses', *Appl. Opt.*, **17**, pp. 1701–1708.

[45] Fienup, J.R. and Leonard, C.D., 1979, 'Holographic optics for a matched-filter optical processor', *Appl. Opt.*, **18**, pp. 631–640.

[46] Kedmi, J. and Friesem, A.A., 1984, 'Optimal holographic Fourier transform lens', *Appl. Opt.*, **23**, pp. 4015–4019.

[47] Upatnieks, J., 1983, 'Portable real-time coherent optical correlator', *Appl. Opt.*, **22**, pp. 2798–2803.

[48] Caimi, F. *et al.*, 1980, 'Laser diode lensless MSF-HOE correlator', *Appl. Opt.*, **19**, pp. 2653–2654.

[49] Grumman Aerospace Corporation, 1975, Final report RE-512 on contract DAAK 02-74-C-0275.

[50] Gara, A.D., 1977, 'Real-time optical correlation of 3D scenes', *Appl. Opt.*, **16**, pp. 149–153.

[51] Gara, A.D., 1979, 'Real-time tracking of moving objects by optical correlation', *Appl. Opt.*, **18**, pp. 172–174.

[52a] Duthie, J.G. *et al.*, 1980, 'Real-time optical correlation with solid-state sources', *Proc. SPIE*, **231**, pp. 281–290.

[52b] Sloan, J. and Udomkesmalee, S., 'An optical processor for object recognition and tracking' (to be published in *Appl. Opt.*).

[53] Duthie, J.G. and Upatnieks, J., 1984, 'Compact real-time coherent optical correlators', *Opt. Eng.*, **23**, pp. 7–11.

[54a] Gibson, D.G. *et al.*, 1984, 'Automatic recognition and tracking of targets from visible or thermal imagery, using optical processing', *Proc. SPIE*, **492**, pp. 165–174.

[54b] Joyeux, D. and Lowenthal, S., 1982, 'Optical Fourier transform: what is the optimal setup?', *Appl. Opt.*, **21**, pp. 4368–4372.

[54c] Wynne, C.G., 1974, 'Simple Fourier transform lenses', *Opt. Comm.*, **12**, pp. 266–274.

[54d] Swantner, W., 1976, 'Lenses for coherent processing', *IEEE Int. Optical Computing Conference*.

[55] Fisher, A.D. and Lee, J.N., 1986, 'The current status of two-dimensional spatial light modulator technology', *Proc. SPIE*, **634**, pp. 352–371.

[56] Casasent, D., 1979, 'Performance evaluation of spatial light modulators', *Appl. Opt.*, **18**, pp. 2445–2453.

[57] Data sheet from Sumitomo Electric Europe S.A., London.

[58] Lipson, S.G. and Nisenson, P., 1974, 'Imaging characteristics of the Itek PROM', *Appl. Opt.*, **13**, pp. 2052–2060.

[59] Petrov, M.P. *et al.*, 1981, 'The PRIZ image converter and its use in optical data processing systems', *Sov. Phys. Tech. Phys.*, **26**, pp. 816–821.

[60a] Casasent, D. *et al.*, 1981, 'Test and evaluation of the Soviet Prom and Priz spatial light modulators', *Appl. Opt.*, **20**, pp. 4215–4220.

[60b] Nilius, M.E. *et al.*, 1986, 'The AFIT PRIZ', *Proc. SPIE*, **639**, pp. 34–40.

[61] Roach, W.R., 1974, 'Resolution of electrooptic light valves', *IEEE Trans. El. Dev.*, **21**, pp. 453–459.

[62] Owechko, Y. and Tanguay Jr., A.R., 1984. 'Theoretical resolution limitations of electrooptic spatial light modulators', *J. Opt. Soc. Am.*, **1A**, pp. 635–643; pp. 644–652.

[63] Bleha, W.P. *et al.*, 1978, 'Application of the light valve to real-time optical data processing', *Opt. Eng.*, **17**, pp. 371–384.

[64] Efron, U. *et al.*, 1983, 'Silicon liquid crystal light valves: status and issues', *Proc. SPIE*, **388**, pp. 75–84.

[65] Sikharulidze, D.G. *et al.*, 1979, 'Liquid-crystal noncoherent–coherent image converter based on a semiconductor-insulator structure', *Sov. J. Qu. Elect.*, **9**, pp. 747–750.

[66] Kompanets, I.N. *et al.*, 1979, 'Spatial modulation of light in a photosensitive structure composed of a liquid crystal and an insulated Gallium Arsenide crystal', *Sov. J. Qu. Elect.*, **9**, pp. 1070–1071.

[67] Dumarevskii, Yu.D. *et al.*, 1984, 'Metal-insulator-semiconductor-liquid crystal structures. Influence of parameters of control signals on characteristics of spatial modulation of light', *Sov. J. Qu. Elect.*, **14**, pp. 493–496.

[68] Baillie, W.L., 'Developments of reflection mode liquid crystal light valves using $Bi_{12}SiO_{20}$ as the photoconductor' (to be published in *IEE Proc. Pt. J.*).

[69] Auborg, P. *et al.*, 1982, 'Liquid crystal light valve using bulk monocrystalline $Bi_{12}SiO_{20}$ as the photoconductive material', *Appl. Opt.*, **21**, pp. 3706–3712.

[70] Ashley, P.R. and Davis, J.H., 1987, 'Amorphous silicon photoconductor in a liquid crystal spatial light modulator', *Appl. Opt.*, **26**, pp. 241–246.

[71] Kiessling, A. *et al.*, 1979, 'An incoherent-to-coherent optical image converter and its application to hybrid optical processors', *European Space Agency J.*, **3**, pp. 185–193.

[72] Poisson, F., 1972, 'Nematic liquid crystal used as an instantaneous holographic medium', *Opt. Comm.*, **6**, pp. 43–44.

[73] Margerum, J.D. *et al.*, 1971, 'Transparent phase images in photoactivated liquid crystals', *App. Phys. Lett.*, **19**, pp. 216–218.

[74] Hass, W.E.L. and Dir, G.A., 1976, 'Simple real-time light valves', *Appl. Phys. Lett.*, **29**, pp. 325–328.

[75] Haas, W.E.L. *et al.*, 1976, 'Ultralow-voltage image intensifiers', *Appl. Phys. Lett.*, **29**, pp. 631–632.

[76] Basyaeva, L.I. *et al.*, 1983, 'Spatial and temporal light modulator of the photo-semiconductor-liquid crystal type exhibiting texture and cholesteric-nematic transitions', *Sov. J. Qu. Elect.*, **13**, pp. 1015–1017.

[77] White, H., British Aerospace, Filton, Bristol, UK (personal communication).

[78] Blinov, M.L., 1983, *Electro-optical and Magneto-optical Properties of Liquid Crystals*, Wiley-Interscience.

[79] Grinberg, J. and Jacobson, A.D., 1976, 'Transmission characteristics of a twisted nematic liquid-crystal layer', *J. Opt. Soc. Am.*, **66**, pp. 1003–1009.

[80] Loiseaux, B. *et al.*, 1985, 'Dynamic optical cross-correlator using a liquid crystal light valve and a bismuth silicon oxide crystal in the Fourier plane', *Opt. Eng.*, **24**, pp. 144–149.

[81] Collings, N. *et al.*, 1987, 'A hybrid optical/electronic image correlator', in *Laser/Optoelectronics in Engineering*, (W. Waidelich, ed.), Springer-Verlag.

[82] Marie, G. *et al.*, 1974, 'Pockel-effect imaging devices and their applications', in *Advances in Image Pickup and Display Devices*, (B. Kazan, ed.), Academic Press.

[83] Maldonado, J.R. and Anderson, L.K., 1971, 'Strain-biased ferroelectric-photoconductor image storage and display devices operated in a reflection mode', *IEEE Trans. Elect. Dev.*, **18**, pp. 774–777.

[84] Armitage, D. *et al.*, 1985, 'High-speed spatial light modulator', *IEEE J. Qu. Elect.*, **21**, pp. 1241–1247.

[85] Kermisch, D., 1976, 'Image formation mechanism in the γ-ruticon', *Appl. Opt.*, **15**, pp. 1775–1786.

[86] Lakatos, A.I. and Bergen, R.F., 1977, 'TV projection display using an amorphous-selenium-type ruticon light valve', *IEEE Trans. Elect. Dev.*, **24**, pp. 930–934.

[87] Fisher, A.D. *et al.*, 1986, 'Photoemitter membrane light modulator', *Opt. Eng.*, **25**, pp. 261–268.

[88] Warde, C. and Thackara, J., 1983, 'Materials limitations of the microchannel spatial light modulator', *Proc. SPIE*, **388**, pp. 96–105.

[89] Hamamatsu product bulletin PB-146, December 1985.

[90] Litton product bulletin.

[91] Ross, W.E. *et al.*, 1983, 'Two-dimensional magneto-optic spatial light modulator for signal processing', *Opt. Eng.*, **22**, pp. 485–490.

[92] Psaltis, D. *et al.*, 1984, 'Optical image correlation with a binary spatial light modulator', *Opt. Eng.*, **23**, pp. 698–704.

[93] Hill, B., 1982, 'Magneto-optic light switching arrays and their application', *J. Non-Cryst. Solids*, **47**, pp. 227–238.

[94] Land, C.E., 1978, 'Optical information storage and spatial light modulation in PLZT ceramics', *Opt. Eng.*, **17**, pp. 317–326.

[95] Lee, S.H. *et al.*, 1986, 'Two-dimensional silicon/PLZT spatial light modulators: design considerations and technology', *Opt. Eng.*, **25**, pp. 250–260.

[96] Takeda, Y., 1974, 'Digital spatial modulators', *Appl. Opt.*, **13**, pp. 825–831.

[97] Pape, D.R. and Hornbeck, L.J., 1983, 'Characteristics of the deformable mirror device for optical information processing', *Proc. SPIE*, **388**, pp. 65–74.

[98] Pape, D.R., 1984, 'An optically addressed membrane spatial light modulator', *Proc. SPIE*, **465**, pp. 17–22.

[99] Brooks, R.E., 1984, 'Micromechanical light modulators for data transfer and processing', *Proc. SPIE*, **465**, pp. 46–54.

[100] Casasent, D., 1978, 'E-beam DKDP light valves', *Opt. Eng.*, **17**, pp. 344–352.

[101] Noble, M.L., 1979, 'Coherent light valve optical modulator', *IEEE Optical Computing Conference* (CH1305-2/79), pp. 5–16.

[102] Laeri, F. *et al.*, 1980, 'Spatial light modulator based on a deformable oil layer', *Opt. Comm.*, **34**, pp. 23–28.

[103] Doyle, R.J. and Glenn, W.E., 1971, 'Lumatron: A high-resolution storage and projection display device', *IEEE Trans. Elect. Dev.*, **18**, pp. 739–747.

[104] Kogelnik, H., 1969, 'Coupled wave theory for thick hologram gratings', *Bell Syst. Tech. J.*, **48**, pp. 2909–2947.

[105] Bage, M.J. and Beddoes, M.P., 1976, 'Parallel matched filtering: minimization of the volume effect', *Appl. Opt.*, **15**, pp. 2632–2634.

[106] Douklias, N. and Shamir, J., 1973, 'Relation between object position and autocorrelation spots in the Vander Lugt filtering process. 2: Influence of the volume nature of the photographic emulsion', *Appl. Opt.*, **12**, pp. 364–367.

[107] Smith, H. (ed.), 1977, *Holographic Recording Materials*, Topics in Applied Physics vol. 20, Springer-Verlag.

[108] Hariharan, P., 1980. 'Holographic recording materials: recent developments', *Opt. Eng.*, **19**, pp. 636–641.

[109] Vijaya Kumar, B.V.K. and Casasent, D., 1980, 'Non-linear t-E curve effects in an optical correlator', *Opt. Comm.*, **34**, pp. 4–6.

[110] Burkhardt, C.B., 1967, 'Storage capacity of an optically formed spatial filter for character recognition', *Appl. Opt.*, **6**, pp. 1359–1366.

[111] Graube, A., 1974, 'Advances in bleaching methods for photographically recorded holograms', *Appl. Opt.*, **13**, pp. 2942–2946.

[112] Calixto, S. and Lessard, R.A., 1984, 'Real-time holography with undeveloped dichromated gelatin films', *Appl. Opt.*, **23**, pp. 1989–1994.

[113] Meier, R.W., 1965, 'Magnification and third-order aberrations in holography', *J. Opt. Soc. Am.*, **55**, pp. 987–992.

[114] Chang, B.J., 1980, 'Dichromated gelatin holograms and their applications', *Opt. Eng.*, **19**, pp. 642–648.

[115] Gregory, D.A. and Liu, H.K., 1984, 'Large-memory real-time multichannel multiplexed pattern recognition', *Appl. Opt.*, **23**, pp. 4560–4570.

[116] Ingwall, R.T. and Fielding, H.L., 1985, 'Hologram recording with a new photopolymer system', *Opt. Eng.*, **24**, pp. 808–811.

[117] Todorov, T. *et al.*, 1984, 'Photopolymers-holographic investigations, mechanism of recording and applications', *Opt. and Quant. Elect.*, **16**, pp. 471–476.

[118] Heller, H.G., 1978, 'The development of photochromic compounds for use in optical information stores', *Chem. and Ind.*, March, pp. 193–196.

[119] Kirkby, C.J., Plessey, Caswell, Northants, UK (personal communication).

[120] Casasent, D. and Caimi, F., 1976, 'Adaptive photodichroic matched spatial filter', *Appl. Opt.*, **15**, p. 2631.

[121] Collins, W.C., 1979, 'Photodichroics as active devices for optical correlation', *Proc. SPIE*, **202**, pp. 132–136.

[122] Friesem, A.A., 1980, 'Photoconductor-thermoplastic devices for holographic nondestructive testing', *Opt. Eng.*, **19**, pp. 659–665.

[123] Minemoto, T. and Nonami, T., 1983, 'Recording a binary computer-generated hologram on a thermoplastic film', *Opt. Comm.*, **47**, pp. 97–100.

[124] Merkle, F. *et al.*, 1980, 'Microprocessor-controlled photo-thermoplastic device for recording and positioning of holographic matched filters', *Proc. SPIE*, **236**, pp. 126–130.

[125] HRC-110 Holo Recorder (Rottenkolber).

[126] HC1000 camera (Newport Corporation).

[127] Lee, T.C. *et al.*, 1978, 'Development of thermoplastic-photoconductor tape for optical recording', *Appl. Opt.*, **17**, pp. 2802–2811.

[128] Lee, T.C. *et al.*, 1979, 'Dual-axis joint-Fourier-transform correlator', *Opt. Lett.*, **4**, pp. 121–123.

[129] Lebreton, G. *et al.*, 1985, 'Imaging on thermoplastic films: a new recording technique for a real-time coherent light valve', *Appl. Opt.*, **24**, pp. 450–453.

[130] Huignard, J.P. and Micheron, F., 1976, 'High sensitivity read-write volume holographic storage in $Bi_{12}SiO_{20}$ and $Bi_{12}SiO_{20}$ crystals', *Appl. Phys. Lett.*, **29**, pp. 591–593.

[131] Guenter, P., 1982, 'Holography, coherent light amplification and optical phase conjugation with photorefractive materials', *Phys. Rep.*, **93**, pp. 199–299.

[132] Neurgaonkar, R.R., 1984, 'Tungsten bronze family crystals for optical device applications', *Proc. SPIE*, **465**, pp. 97–101.

[133] Brown, B.R. and Lohmann, A.W., 1966, 'Complex spatial filtering with binary masks', *Appl. Opt.*, **5**, pp. 967–970.

[134] Lohmann, A.W. and Paris, D.P., 1967, 'Binary Fraunhofer holograms, generated by computer', *Appl. Opt.*, **6**, pp. 1739–1748.

[135] Leger, J.R. *et al.*, 1982, 'A microcomputer-based hybrid processor at the University of California, San Diego', *Opt. Eng.*, **21**, pp. 557–564.

[136] Sandstrom, R. and Lee, S.H., 1983, 'Production of optical coordinate transform filters by a computer controlled scanning interferometric scanning system', *Proc. SPIE*, **437**, pp. 64–71.

[137] Caulfield, H.J. *et al.*, 1983, 'Continuous tone holograms by halftoning', *Proc. SPIE*, **437**, pp. 60–63.

[138] Leung, K.M. *et al.*, 1981, 'Using e-beam written computer-generated holograms to test deep aspheric wavefronts', *Proc. SPIE*, **306**, pp. 161–167.

[139] Freyer, J.L. *et al.*, 1983, 'Digital holography: algorithms, e-beam lithography, and 3 D display', *Proc. SPIE*, **437**, pp. 38–47.

[140] Horner, J.L. and Gianino, P.D., 1985, 'Applying the phase-only filter concept to the synthetic discriminant function correlation filter', *Appl. Opt.*, **24**, pp. 851–855.

[141] Lee, W.-H., 1978, 'Computer-generated holograms: techniques and applications', *Progress in Optics* vol. XVI, North-Holland, pp. 121–232.

[142] Allebach, J.P., 1981, 'Representation-related errors in binary digital holograms: a unified analysis', *Appl. Opt.*, **20**, pp. 290–299.

[143] Velzel, C.H.F., 1973, 'Image contrast and efficiency of non-linearly recorded holograms of diffusively reflecting objects', *Opt. Acta*, **20**, pp. 585–606.

[144] Gabel, R.A. and Liu, B., 1970, 'Minimisation of reconstruction errors with computer generated binary holograms', *Appl. Opt.*, **9**, pp. 1180–1191.

[145] Squires, R.H. and Allebach, J.P., 1983, 'Digital holograms: a guide to reducing quantization and phase encoding errors', *Proc. SPIE*, **437**, pp. 12–18.

[146] Gopfert, W.M. and Read, A.A., 1976, 'Optical cross-correlation by complex exponentiation of the input data', *Proc. SPIE*, **83**, pp. 146–153.

[147] Gray, P.F. and Barnett, M.E., 1975, 'Matched filtering of continuous tone transparencies using phase media', *Opt. Comm.*, **14**, pp. 46–50.

[148] Lohmann, A.W. and Thum, C., 1984, 'Increased light efficiency of coherent-optical matched filters', *Appl. Opt.*, **23**, pp. 1503–1508.

[149] Leger, J.R. and Lee, S.H., 1982, 'Hybrid optical processor for pattern recognition and classification using a generalized set of pattern functions', *Appl. Opt.*, **21**, pp. 274–287.

[150] Casasent, D. and Furman, A., 1977, 'Sources of correlation degradation', *Appl. Opt.*, **16**, pp. 1652–1661.

[151] Vander Lugt, A., 1966, 'Practical considerations for the use of spatial carrier-frequency filters', *Appl. Opt.*, **5**, pp. 1760–1765.

[152] Herold, R. and Leib, K., 1977, 'Image rotation in optical correlators through rotational devices', *Grumman Aerospace Corporation Report* #RM-627.

[153] Hara, T. *et al.*, 1986, 'Microchannel spatial light modulator having the functions of image zooming, shifting, and rotating', *Appl. Opt.*, **25**, pp. 2306–2310.

[154] Casasent, D. and Kraus, M., 1978, 'Polar camera for space-variant pattern recognition', *Appl. Opt.*, **17**, pp. 1559–1561.

[155] Casasent, D., 1978, 'Deformation invariant, space-variant optical pattern recognition', *Progress in Optics* vol. XVI, North-Holland, pp. 291–356.

[156] Saito, Y. *et al.*, 1983, 'Scale and rotation invariant real time optical correlator using computer generated hologram', *Opt. Comm.*, **47**, pp. 8–11.

[157] Casasent, D. and Psaltis, D., 1977, 'Space-bandwidth product and accuracy of the optical Mellin transform', *Appl. Opt.*, **16**, p. 1472.

[158] Casasent, D. and Klimas, E., 1978, 'Multichannel optical correlator for radar signal processing', *Appl. Opt.*, **17**, pp. 2058–2063.

[159] Lebreton, G. and de Bazelaire, E., 1980, 'Holographic processing of wideband antenna data', *Opt. Eng.*, **19**, pp. 739–747.

[160] Thomas, C.E., 1966, 'Optical spectrum analysis of large space bandwidth signals', *Appl. Opt.*, **5**, pp. 1782–1790.

[161] Rhodes, W.T., 1981, 'The falling raster in optical signal processing', *Proc. SPIE*, **373**, pp. 11–19.

[162] Barniv, Y. and Casasent, D., 1981, 'Multisensor image registration: experimental verification', *Proc. SPIE*, **292**, pp. 160–171.

[163] Casasent, D. and Munoz, D., 1979, 'Statistical and deterministic aspects of multisensor optical image pattern recognition', *Proc. SPIE*, **210**, pp. 58–64.

[164] Armitage, D. and Thackara, J.I., 1986, 'Liquid-crystal differentiating spatial light modulator', *Proc. SPIE*, **613**, pp. 165–171.

[165] Casasent, D. and Chen, J., 1983, 'Nonlinear local image preprocessing using coherent optical techniques', *Appl. Opt.*, **22**, pp. 808–814.

[166] Casasent, D. and Cheatham, R.L., 1984, 'Image segmentation and real-image tests for an optical moment-based feature extractor', *Opt. Comm.*, **51**, pp. 227–230.

[167] Arsenault, H.H. and Denis, M., 1983, 'Image processing in signal-dependent noise', *Can. J. Phys.*, **61**, pp. 309–317.

[168] Lindstrom, P.G., 1987, *Computer simulation of hybrid cross-correlators*, Ph.D. thesis: University of Manchester Institute of Science and Technology, England.

[169] Fukunaga, K., 1972, *Introduction to Statistical Pattern Recognition*, Academic Press.

[170] Duvernoy, J., 1976, 'Optical pattern recognition and clustering: Karhunen-Loeve analysis', *Appl. Opt.*, **15**, pp. 1584–1590.

[171] Casasent, D. and Sharma, V., 1984, 'Feature extractors for distortion-invariant robot vision', *Opt. Eng.*, **23**, pp. 492–498.

[172] Leger, J.R. and Lee, S.H., 1982, 'Image classification by an optical implementation of the Fukunaga-Koontz transform', *J. Opt. Soc. Am.*, **72**, pp. 556–564.

[173] Gu, Z.-H. *et al.*, 1982, 'Optical implementation of the least-squares linear mapping technique for image classification', *J. Opt. Soc. Am.*, **72**, pp. 787–793.

[174] Gu, Z.-H. and Lee, S.H., 1984, 'Optical implementation of the Hotelling trace criterion for image classification', *Opt. Eng.*, **23**, pp. 727–731.

[175] Girnyk, V.I. *et al.*, 1982, 'Use of digital holographic filters to optimise methods for coherent-optical pattern recognition', *Opt. Spectrosc.*, **52**, pp. 317–320; pp. 622–625.

[176] Braunecker, B. *et al.*, 1979, 'Optical character recognition based on nonredundant correlation measurements', *Appl. Opt.*, **18**, pp. 2746–2753.

[177] Caulfield, H.J., 1981, 'Space invariant composite matched filters for space-variant processors', *Proc. SPIE*, **317**, pp. 164–172.

[178] Caulfield, H.J. and Weinberg, M.H., 1982, 'Computer recognition of 2-D patterns using generalized matched filters', *Appl. Opt.*, **21**, pp. 1699–1704.

[179] Casasent, D., 1984, 'Unified synthetic discriminant function computational formulation', *Appl. Opt.*, **23**, pp. 1620–1627.

[180] Casasent, D. and Sharma, V., 1983, 'Shift-invariant and distortion-invariant object recognition', *Proc. SPIE*, **442**, pp. 47–55.

[181] Casasent, D. *et al.*, 1984, 'Projection SDF performance', *Opt. Eng.*, **23**, pp. 716–720.

[182] Horner, J.L. and Gianino, P.D., 1985, 'Applying the phase-only filter concept to the SDF correlation filter', *Appl. Opt.*, **24**, pp. 851–855.

[183] Riggins, J. and Butler, S., 1984, 'Simulation of SDF optical implementation', *Opt. Eng.*, **23**, pp. 721–726.

[184] Chang, W.-T. *et al.*, 1984, 'SDF control of correlation plane structure for 3D object representation and recognition', *Proc. SPIE*, **507**, pp. 9–18.

[185] Grumet, A., 1972, 'Automatic target recognition system', US patent #3779492.

[186] Gregory, D.A. and Liu, H.K., 1984, 'Large-memory real-time multichannel multiplexed pattern recognition', *Appl. Opt.*, **23**, pp. 4560–4570.

[187] Liu, H.K. and Duthie, J.G., 1982, 'Real-time screen-aided multiple-image optical holographic matched-filter correlator', *Appl. Opt.*, **21**, pp. 3278–3286.

[188] Leib, K.G. and Mendelsohn, J., 'Investigation of large capacity optical memories for correlator applications', *Grumman Research Dept. Report* RE-634 (AFOSR-TR-81-0802).

[189] Nomura, H. and Okoshi, T., 1976, 'Storage density limitation of a volume-type hologram memory: theory', *Appl. Opt.*, **15**, pp. 550–555.

[190] Friesem, A.A. and Walker, J.L., 1970, 'Thick absorption recording media in holography', *Appl. Opt.*, **9**, pp. 201–214.

[191] Hsu, Y.-N. and Arsenault, H.H., 1982, 'Rotation-invariant digital pattern recognition using circular harmonic expansion', *Appl. Opt.*, **21**, pp. 4012–4015.

[192] Dandliker, R. *et al.*, 1983, 'Hybrid coherent optical and electronic object recognition', *Appl. Opt.*, **22**, pp. 2081–2086.

[193] Schils, G.F. and Sweeney, D.W., 1986, 'Rotationally invariant correlation filtering for multiple images', *J. Opt. Soc. Am.*, **3A**, pp. 902–908.

[194] Merkle, F. and Lorch, T., 1984, 'Hybrid optical-digital pattern recognition', *Appl. Opt.*, **23**, pp. 1509–1516.

[195] Pepper, D.M. *et al.*, 1978, 'Spatial convolution and correlation of optical fields via degenerate four-wave mixing', *Opt. Lett.*, **3**, pp. 7–9.

[196] Kukhtarev, N.V. and Odulov, S.G., 1979, 'Wavefront convolution in four-wave interaction in media with nonlocal nonlinearity', *JETP Lett.*, **30**, pp. 6–11.

[197] Odulov, S.G. and Soskin, M.S., 1980, 'Correlation analysis of images under degenerate four-wave mixing in colliding beams', *Sov. Phys. Dok.*, **25**, pp. 380–381.

[198] White, J.O. and Yariv, A., 1980, 'Real-time image processing via four-wave mixing in a photorefractive medium', *App. Phys. Lett.*, **37**, pp. 5–7.

[199] Vander Lugt, A. and Rotz, F.B., 1970, 'The use of film nonlinearities in optical spatial filtering', *Appl. Opt.*, **9**, pp. 215–222.

[200] Indebetouw, G., 1981, 'Optical correlator with extended depth of field', *Opt. Comm.*, **39**, pp. 21–25.

[201] Barnett, M.E. *et al.*, 1976, 'An interactive hybrid processing facility for geological and geographical applications', *Proc. SPIE*, **74**, pp. 130–136.

[202] Lyman, J., 1987, 'Moving wafer inspection into the fast lane', *Electronics*, March 5, pp. 74–77.

[203] Gorstein, M. *et al.*, 1970, 'Two approaches to the star mapping problem for space vehicle attitude determination', *Appl. Opt.*, **9**, pp. 351–358.

[204] Wilson, A.C., 1986, 'Array processors: the best way to process images?', *Digital Design*, January, pp. 47–52.

[205] Fu, K.-S. (ed.), 1984, *VLSI for Pattern Recognition and Image Processing*, Springer-Verlag.

INDEX